SAINTS
of the
BIBLE

Exploring Scripture
with Holy Men and Women

by

THERESA DOYLE-NELSON

Our Sunday Visitor Publishing Division
Our Sunday Visitor, Inc.
Huntington, Indiana 46750

Our Sunday Visitor Publishing Division
Our Sunday Visitor, Inc.
200 Noll Plaza
Huntington, IN 46750

ISBN: 978-1-59276-317-7 (Inventory No. T416)
LCCN: 2008942139

Cover design: Lindsey Luken
Cover image: Shutterstock
Interior design: Sherri L. Hoffman

PRINTED IN THE UNITED STATES OF AMERICA

DEDICATION

This book is dedicated to my very best friend
and husband:

Chad Nelson

And to my three beautiful sons:
Seamus
Ian
Noah

THANK YOU

I thank God with all my heart for insistently
and persistently nudging me into and through the
wonderful journey of writing this book.

*Your word is a lamp to my feet
and a light to my path.*

— Ps. 119:105

CONTENTS

INTRODUCTION

I've always had a great interest in both the Bible and saints, and more than once I'd thought how nice it would be to have a book blending these two topics. I kept my eyes open at bookstores and did thorough online searches, but could never find such a book. Then, as my children got older and I had more time on my hands — and had already begun to enjoy the art of writing — it dawned on me that perhaps I could write a book like this.

The idea of starting this project was rather daunting. But I decided that I could at least put together a list of Bible saint names, just for knowledge's sake. With all of the saint books on my shelves and so much information on the Internet, I figured this task would be easy enough. I was wrong! So many of the resources contradicted one other that the task quickly became very confusing. Finally, I decided to use a copy of *Butler's Lives of the Saints* to create the list of Bible saints. I then felt strongly compelled to keep moving. I began digging, delving, searching, writing, and rewriting (and rewriting, and rewriting . . .) on each saint — and this is the result.

The saints you find in this book are arranged according to the feast days they have been assigned by the Church, starting with Mary on January 1 and ending with The Holy Innocents on December 28. Each Bible saint entry is followed by a cluster of Bible verses. These verses offer additional spots in the Bible where you can read more about each particular saint, or learn some relevant information. All of the saints included are official — with one odd exception.

After recently acquiring a copy of the most up-to-date Roman Martyrology (the true "horse's mouth" on Catholic saints, I've learned), I discovered Jason was no longer listed as a saint! However, because his story is so intriguing and he was considered to be a saint for so long, I compromised: I took away the title of "saint," but left Jason's story in the book.

I hope you find the information in this book to be interesting and thought-provoking. I hope you enjoy reading about these wonderful individuals and considering the impact their lives have had on the Church.

THE BLESSED MOTHER MARY

January 1
Patroness of Motherhood, Nuns, Aviators;
Protection During Storms

And the angel said to her, "Do not be afraid, Mary, for you have found favor with God. And behold, you will conceive in your womb and bear a son, and you shall call his name Jesus."

— LK. 1:30-31

Mary is a phenomenally popular saint in both the Catholic Church and other faiths. People seem to feel a special closeness and warm affection toward her. Reading the Bible makes it easy to understand why. Each story in the New Testament involving Mary presents a woman full of tenderness, compassion, and quiet humility, completely lacking any sense of arrogance or rudeness.

The main narratives in the Bible that help us better understand and love Mary tell of rich, thought-provoking events: the circumstances of Jesus's birth, the dramatic finding of the child Jesus in the Temple, asking Jesus for help at the wedding at Cana, the Crucifixion, and praying with the apostles in the Upper Room after Jesus's death and ascension.

All of these chronicles demonstrate her perfect willingness to please God, even though logically she must have felt confusion, terror, and extreme sadness at times. They all illustrate her sense of calm, love, and gentleness, as a mother and as a person.

The Rosary is a beloved prayer for those with a keen devotion to Mary. Although the Rosary encompasses many prayers, the "Hail Mary" is the largest part of the devotion; it is a meditative prayer derived almost entirely from the Gospel of Luke, with a plea to Mary for prayers at the end.

Mary seems to have taken all of humankind on as her own children. Through her many apparitions over the centuries, she has delivered countless messages for all of humankind — messages of love, prayer, peace, and hope. Among her better-known apparitions are those of Fatima (Portugal), Lourdes (France), and Mexico City.

With Mary's appealing and mystic expressions of love and interest, numerous feast days have evolved to celebrate the many aspects of Our Blessed Mother. Jan. 1, one of the older feast days, commemorates her motherhood. Other feast days include Sept. 8, which honors Mary's birthday, and Oct. 7, the feast of Our Lady of the Rosary.

Lk. 1:39-45 • Mt. 2:1-12 • Lk. 2:41-52 • Jn. 2:1-11
Jn. 19:25-27 • Acts 1:13-14

ST. TIMOTHY

January 26
Patron of Stomach Disorder Sufferers

And he came also to Derbe and to Lystra. A disciple was there, named Timothy, the son of a Jewish woman who was a believer; but his father was a Greek. He was well spoken of by the brethren at Lystra and Iconium. Paul wanted Timothy to accompany him . . .

— ACTS 16:1-3

Paul's first missionary visit to Lystra (located in present-day Turkey) must have struck its resident Timothy in a powerful way, because by the time Paul made a return visit, Timothy was known as an inspiring and influential person within the Christian community there. Timothy's grasp of the new Faith must have been remarkable and profound, because he quickly became one of Paul's closest disciples and a truly gifted missionary companion and assistant.

It is clear from several mentions throughout the epistles that Timothy spent much time with Paul, helping to spread the way of Christ. Paul's plentiful references to Timothy are full of respect and warmth: "My beloved and faithful son in the Lord," "I have no one comparable to him," "My true child in faith," and the like.

Although Timothy's mother was Jewish, his father was a Gentile, and so not all Jewish customs were followed during his childhood. Timothy made great efforts to work with

Judaizers — Jewish Christians who insisted that all converts to Christianity (Gentiles included) embrace the multitude of demanding and difficult Jewish laws. Timothy even underwent circumcision to appease these people.

In the midst of their varied missionary travels, Timothy ultimately stayed in Ephesus and became the first bishop there. While developing the Christian community in Ephesus, Timothy received two letters believed to have been written by Paul; they are now known as 1 and 2 Timothy in the Bible. These letters offered sound advice, encouragement, and inspiration. 1 and 2 Timothy (along with the epistle to Titus) are often referred to as "pastoral letters" because they give wonderful advice on how to pastor, or lead, a church. These letters, combined with Timothy's own enthusiastic spirit, gave Ephesus a strong start as one of the earliest Christian communities.

Although historical accounts are not clear, it is believed that Timothy spent the rest of his life in Ephesus and was ultimately stoned to death during a pagan festival near the year A.D. 97.

1 Cor. 4:17 · 1 Cor. 16:10 · 1 Thess. 3:1-6
1 Tim. 1:18-20 · 2 Tim. 1:1-5

ST. TITUS

January 26
Patron of Crete

For even when we came into Macedonia, our bodies had no rest but we were afflicted at every turn — fighting without and fear within. But God, who comforts the downcast, comforted us by the coming of Titus.

— 2 COR. 7:5-6

Titus was a Gentile, from a Greek family, with no connection to Judaism. So, although he never anxiously awaited the "Messiah," through the influence of Paul, Titus found Christianity to be a compelling way of life; he soon became a moving force behind the initial spread of Christianity.

While it was Paul who inspired and converted Titus, before long it was Titus who brought assistance and comfort to Paul. Near A.D. 49, Titus accompanied Paul a meeting in Jerusalem, most likely the "Council of Jerusalem," as described in Acts 15. The two brethren were able to help these leaders understand the insignificance and detriment of forcing Gentile Christian converts to comply with the overwhelming demands of the Mosaic Law.

Titus was also very helpful in the mid-50s A.D., when Paul encountered arguments, false teachings, strife, and confusion in the new church in Corinth. Paul struggled to guide the Corinthians peacefully and with ease, while Titus seemed to have the right inspiration, words, and actions to bring about the unity needed to help solidify this brand-new way of life and faith in Corinth.

Eventually, Paul sent Titus to the Mediterranean island of Crete to build up the new faith there; this made Titus the first bishop of Crete. While there, Paul (or a disciple of his) sent him a letter filled with encouragement, advice, and blessings for Titus's fervent endeavors there. This is now known as the epistle to Titus, one of those epistles labeled "pastoral letters." It has evolved into a special sort of document that offers guidance on solid ways to pastor a church. The book of Titus still offers sound and helpful advice to Church leaders.

Titus died a peaceful death at an old age, circa A.D. 96.

---

2 Cor. 2:13 · 2 Cor. 8:16-19, 23 · Gal. 2:1- 3 · Titus 1:4-5

HOLY SIMEON

February 3
(Formerly October 8)
Patron of the Elderly

Now there was a man in Jerusalem, whose name was Simeon, and this man was righteous and devout, looking for the consolation of Israel, and the holy Spirit was upon him.

— LK. 2:25

Holy Simeon's story beautifully illustrates the rewards of having patience and trust in the Lord.

Simeon, known for his piety and unyielding devotion to God, lived during the time of Jesus's birth and is written about in Luke's Gospel. Luke tells us that Simeon had been blessed with a special promise from the Holy Spirit — that he would not die until his eyes rested upon the Messiah of Israel. As time went on, he eagerly anticipated that pledged encounter.

Joseph and Mary were devout Jews, conscientious about following the Mosaic Law. According to the regulations written out in Leviticus, Mary waited 40 days after the birth of Jesus, and then with Joseph brought the baby to be presented at the Temple in Jerusalem in order to consecrate him to the Lord. Because they were not of great wealth, Mary and Joseph brought two turtledoves (or perhaps pigeons) instead of a yearling lamb as an offering.

Simeon was at the Temple when Jesus, Mary, and Joseph arrived. When he met the Holy Family, he gathered the baby Jesus into his arms and somehow knew that this was Whom he'd been waiting for. The Holy Spirit stirred his soul, confirming to him that the promise was at that moment being fulfilled. Without a doubt, he was holding Israel's redeemer.

Simeon, overcome with wonder and awe, fell into heartfelt prayer, expressing a certain readiness for death, now that he had indeed seen the Savior of the world. Simeon also included a prophecy: this Savior would be a glory for Israel as well as a light for the Gentiles, thereby opening the doors of salvation to all people.

Mary and Joseph were astonished at Simeon's prayer. As the holy man blessed the couple, he prophesied about future upheavals for Israel and future sorrows for Mary, being the mother of Jesus.

Lk. 2:22-35 • Lev. 12:1-8

ST. ONESIMUS THE SLAVE

February 15
(Formerly February 16)
Patron of Discouraged Employees

I appeal to you for my child, Onesimus, whose father I have become in my imprisonment. (Formerly he was useless to you, but now he is indeed useful to you and to me.) I am sending him back to you, sending my very heart.

— PHILEM. 10-12

If you have ever felt overworked and underpaid, or have had a desire to become somewhat of a "slave" to God, St. Onesimus might pique your interest. Although Onesimus is not mentioned a great deal in the New Testament, his story is touching.

Onesimus was a slave to one of the early Christians in Colossae. Understandably, Onesimus felt discouraged with his "job" and wanted a better life, so he ran away. He somehow managed to meet up with an imprisoned Paul, either in Ephesus or Rome — indications in the Bible are not clear. Paul, with his amazing understanding and ability to evangelize, first managed to convince Onesimus to embrace Christianity, then to return to his earthly master, Philemon. Paul sent a personal letter to Philemon along with Onesimus, encouraging forgiveness and acceptance towards the slave. This letter became known as the epistle of Philemon. It has a very tender touch to it. You can feel Paul's gentle nudge towards tolerance and equality.

There is a slight hint to a more relaxed side of Paul in this letter to Philemon. The name *Onesimus* is Greek for "useful." Paul plays on that word, pointing out to Philemon how Onesimus was for a time "useless" but had become "useful" since his conversion to Christianity.

The letter must have worked, because Tradition tells us that Philemon did not punish Onesimus upon his return, as would have been the norm, but apparently sent his slave back to Paul. Onesimus went from being a slave to an earthly master to a slave for God. Surely, he was wonderful and helpful to Paul in establishing the roots of Catholicism.

Evidently, many early Church leaders felt a connection with this former slave and decided to use the name "Onesimus" as a religious name. Although this caused confusion for earlier historians as to which Onesimus was which, the fact that a number of religious took on his name speaks volumes.

It is believed that Onesimus was martyred about A.D. 90.

Col. 4:9 · Philem. 10-17 · Col. 3:22-25

ST. JOSEPH

March 19
Patron of Fathers, Workers,
A Peaceful Death

But as he considered this, behold, an angel of the Lord appeared to him in a dream, saying, "Joseph, son of David, do not fear to take Mary your wife, for that which is conceived in her is of the Holy Spirit; she will bear a son, and you shall call his name Jesus . . ."

— MT. 1:20-21

God, the true father of Jesus, desired to have an earthly father for His Son as well. God chose a gentle, quiet, and humble man named Joseph, a carpenter from Nazareth who was actually already betrothed to Mary. When he discovered that Mary was with child, before he had brought her into his home, he was stunned. He agonized over what to do. He wondered how he could marry her when he knew the child was not his. Because of his caring and righteous nature, he decided to divorce her quietly in order to avoid humiliating her publicly. However, in a dream, an angel told Joseph not to worry, that the child was conceived by the Holy Spirit, and that Joseph was needed to be the foster father of the baby. Joseph immediately canceled his plans of divorce and took Mary into his home.

This is the first evidence of Joseph's calm, considerate, and God-fearing nature, one we see throughout New Testament narratives. The examples are many:

- Joseph carefully took Mary to Bethlehem when a census was ordered.
- He was at Mary's and Jesus's side during the visits of the shepherds and Magi.
- He was a quiet and, no doubt, an amazed witness when Jesus was presented to Simeon at the Temple.
- He paid heed to more dreams from the angel of the Lord, taking Mary and Baby Jesus to Egypt to escape the wrath of Herod, and then returning to Nazareth when it was safe.
- Finally, the last mention of Joseph is that he anxiously helped Mary search for Jesus for three days in the hectic city of Jerusalem.

Joseph's nature offers inspiration for a strong, quiet confidence in the Lord. There is never a sense of chaos or disarray about him. Even when he didn't understand what was happening and things seemed illogical, he completely trusted and let God guide him.

Lk. 2:1-7 · Lk. 2:15-16 · Lk. 2:33 · Mt. 2:13-15
Mt. 2:19-23 · Lk. 2:41-52

ST. DISMAS THE GOOD THIEF

March 25
Patron of Prisoners, Repentant Thieves, Penitent Criminals

"And we indeed justly; for we are receiving the due reward of our deeds; but this man has done nothing wrong." And he said, "Jesus, remember me when you come in your kingly power."
— LK. 23:41-42

All four of the Gospels acquaint readers with the two criminals/revolutionaries crucified with Jesus. However, it is Luke who gives us an interesting peek into their personalities. His story has caused many believers to feel drawn to the one some early Christians named "Dismas" (Greek for "dying").

Dismas was uniquely sobered during his crucifixion. As he considered his situation, while up on his own cross, he became — in a unique way — awash in humility and regret. This newfound humbleness seemed to spur on a new hope, trust, faith, and love. After Gestas (the name given to the criminal hung on the other side of Jesus) reviled Jesus, demanding that Jesus do something about their precarious situation, it was Dismas who admonished him, who stepped in and defended Jesus. It was Dismas who reminded him that they had done wrong. They deserved their punishments. Dismas was clear in pointing out to Gestas that Jesus was an innocent man and did not deserve to be the recipient of such loathsome abuse, much less subjected to a crucifixion.

As the heart and mind of Dismas lightened, he came to know that he was next to a man of overwhelming love and power and decided to risk asking Jesus for an undeserved, glorious favor: that Jesus would remember him when Jesus arrived at His kingdom. Jesus's response was striking — a promise that they would be together that very day in Paradise! This phenomenal pledge probably made the pain of Dismas's crucifixion seem less horrific, perhaps even joyful, on that traumatic day. Jesus's forgiving Dismas with such ease, even though he had been a great sinner, is a wonderful sign of hope and encouragement for all.

Mt. 27:38, 44 • Mk. 15:27, 32 • Lk. 23:33, 39-43 • Jn. 19:18

ST. MARY OF CLOPAS

April 24
(Formerly April 9)
Patron of Caretakers

But standing by the cross of Jesus were his mother, and his mother's sister, Mary the wife of Clopas, and Mary Magdalene.

— JN. 19:25

Due to the sheer number of Marys in the New Testament, it takes extra care to pick out Mary, the wife of Clopas, and clearly see her role in Jesus's life. By examining and comparing the Crucifixion scene as described by the different Gospel writers, most biblical historians have concluded that the Mary of Clopas found in John's Gospel was likely the same as "Mary the mother of James and Joseph" found in Matthew's Crucifixion narration, as well as "Mary the mother of the younger James and of Joses" found in Mark's version. Mark further explains that Mary of Clopas was one of the women from Galilee who had often accompanied Jesus during his mission and assisted him in his works.

After despondently viewing the death of their Lord, Mary of Clopas and her Christian sisters wanted to anoint Jesus's body with spices. However, the Sabbath was rapidly approaching, so the women put the anointing on hold until very early Sunday morning, when they went to the tomb to tend to the chore. As Mary of Clopas, Mary Magdalene, and Salome approached the tomb, they were startled to see that the stone had already been moved. As they entered the tomb, they were further amazed to see an angel of God sitting at the tomb. This angel told the women that Jesus had been raised and instructed them to go tell the disciples that Jesus was alive.

Trembling with fear and elation, Mary of Clopas and her friends rushed off to share the miraculous news . . . only to meet Jesus on their way to see the disciples! Overwhelmed with love and bliss, they fell to their knees and embraced His feet. Jesus eased their anxieties and gave them the encouragement they needed to confidently proclaim this good news, and they rushed to tell the disciples all that had happened.

Although Mary of Clopas's name is not mentioned again in Scripture, it is likely that she was present with the many other followers of Christ at Pentecost.

Mt. 27:56, 61 • Mt. 28:1-10 • Mk. 15:40-41, 47
Mk. 16:1-8 • Lk. 24:10

ST. MARK THE EVANGELIST

April 25
Patron of Lawyers, Venice, Stained Glass Workers

Get Mark and bring him with you; for he is very useful in serving me.

— 2 TIM. 4:11B

Mark, also known as John Mark, does not specifically appear in any of the Gospels. However, we learn a fair bit about him in the book of Acts. Evidently, he was a very early Christian filled with great faith. Mark's mother, Mary, was also a devout believer in Christ, frequently letting her home be used as a gathering place for the early Church members in Jerusalem.

Mark's zest for Christ must have struck Paul in a profound way, because he asked Mark to go on an ambitious missionary journey with him and Barnabas. In the midst of their travels, however, Mark abruptly left the others; the Bible never gives a reason why, and readers can only guess, but it is clear that his leaving caused some serious tension. While Paul and Barnabas were planning another missionary voyage, they disagreed intensely over whether Mark should join them. While Barnabas firmly defended Mark, Paul was skeptical about his earlier abandonment, and their discord caused them to split.

In the end, however, it is clear that the distrust Paul felt toward Mark was eventually replaced with respect and friendship. He wrote in his second letter to Timothy that he desired to see Mark because Mark was helpful.

Besides helping the faith grow at home and abroad, Mark also wrote the second Gospel. Mark's Gospel has a few unique characteristics to it. It is the shortest of all the Gospels, with a very plain writing style, and seems to be written after much interaction with Peter. Mark's Gospel stresses the divinity of Jesus, by putting a strong emphasis on His miracles.

Many historians believe that after writing the Gospel, Mark moved to Alexandria, Egypt, and became the first bishop there. Although the cause and date of his death are uncertain, most believe that he was martyred. There is also a strong tradition that the people of Venice obtained the remains of his body in the ninth century and brought them to Venice. There, they constructed a stunning cathedral to hold his relics — San Marco — where St. Mark has been venerated for centuries.

Acts 12:12 • Acts 12:25 • Acts 13:5, 13
Acts 15:37-39 • Col. 4:10

ST. SIMON OF JERUSALEM

April 27
(Formerly February 18)
Patron of Bishops

"Is not this the carpenter's son? Is not his mother called Mary? And are not his brethren James, and Joseph and Simon, and Judas?"
— MT. 13:55

According to the Bible, Simon was one of the "brothers" of Jesus. However, it is important to understand the meaning of the word *brother* as it was understood over 2,000 years ago in Galilee. Families were very close-knit — cousins, aunts, and uncles were often considered to be a part of the immediate family. Dear friends or close neighbors could also be regarded as "family." Therefore, the term "brother," when used in the Biblical sense, has a very broad definition; Simon was likely connected to Jesus in some way other than the strictest sense of the word "brother." He was perhaps a cousin or close family friend. Evidently, Simon was also from Nazareth and likely spent a fair amount of his childhood with or near Jesus. Some scholars claim that Simon's father was the Cleopas mentioned in Luke's Gospel.

Although Simon is merely mentioned in the Bible, and no stories on him are offered, historical resources tell us more. When James, the first bishop of Jerusalem, was martyred in A.D. 62, some apostles and disciples gathered together to select a new bishop for the city, and chose this relative of Christ.

Simon proved himself to be a good shepherd to the early Christians of Jerusalem. Prior to the destruction of the Temple in Jerusalem in A.D. 70, the Church there purportedly received a divine warning of the doom about to come, and Simon moved the Christians of the city to Pella, a small town across the Jordan River. After the danger had passed, he brought his flock back; Jerusalem was devastated, but its community of Christians was spared. Upon their return, Christianity experienced a time of growth and strengthening within Jerusalem.

Unfortunately, the enemies of Christians and Jews in Jerusalem ultimately caught up with Simon. Sometime near A.D. 107, Emperor Trajan ordered a death sentence for all people of these faiths in the city, and Simon was captured. Even though he was quite elderly by this time, Tradition claims that he bravely withstood wicked torture and was then crucified.

Simon had already inspired a great love for Jesus throughout the region, however, and his death could not stop the wide ripple effect of his wondrous faith and deeds.

Mt. 12:46-50 · Mt. 13:54-58 · Mk. 6:1-6 · Lk. 24:18

ST. JAMES THE LESS

May 3
Patron of Pharmacists,
Unnoticed People

And when they entered, they went up to the upper room, where they were staying, Peter and John and James and Andrew, Philip and Thomas, Bartholomew and Matthew, James son of Alphaeus and Simon the Zealot and Judas the son of James. All these with one accord devoted themselves to prayer . . .

— ACTS 1:13-14A

St. James the Less is known as "James, son of Alphaeus" in the Bible. Because there are so many references to the name of James in the Bible, it becomes a bit of a challenge to figure out exactly who this James was. All that is known with certainty is that he was one of Jesus's twelve apostles, and that his father's name was Alphaeus.

The title of James the "Less" can be confusing and misleading. Chances are that he was either smaller in size, younger in age, or merely called to be an apostle later than James the Greater. Assuming that his work and life were of "less" value than that of James the Greater, however, has little basis in fact.

The biggest clue in supposing more about James the Less is in the name of his father, Alphaeus. For example, the Gospel of Mark tells us that the apostle Matthew (also known as Levi) had a father named Alphaeus as well. From this knowledge, one could consider the possibility that Matthew/Levi and James the Less were brothers.

Another point to ponder is that the name Alphaeus is often considered to be Aramaic for the Greek name of Clopas. Therefore, it becomes credible that James the Less was the son of Mary of Clopas. If this James was indeed a son of Mary of Clopas (who did in fact have a son named James), we would know that he had a brother named Joses (or Joseph). Some have also suggested that the father of James the Less, Alphaeus, might be the Cleopas who met up with, yet didn't immediately recognize, Jesus on the road to Emmaus. It is not certain, but plausible, that the differences in spelling (Clopas vs. Cleopas) could be attributed to two separate authors using different spellings.

James the Less is considered by many (but not all) to be the same as James the Just, who became the much-loved first bishop of Jerusalem and attended the Council of Jerusalem, as described in Acts.

Mt. 10:3 · Mk. 2:14 · Mk. 15:40
Lk. 24:18 · Acts 15:13-20

ST. PHILIP THE APOSTLE

May 3
Patron of Hatmakers, Pastry Chefs

The next day Jesus decided to go to Galilee. And he found Philip and said to him, "Follow me."

— JN. 1:43

While Matthew, Mark, and the Acts of the Apostles merely list Philip as one of the twelve apostles, John's Gospel gives some more intriguing insights. According to John's Gospel, Philip was one of the first few apostles to be called. He seemed to have no feeling of doubt; following Jesus was the right thing to do. He even sought out his friend Nathanael right away to share the exciting news with him.

Although Philip initially accepted Jesus as the Messiah with ease, and freely followed Him, there are a few hints later on in John's Gospel that illustrate a lack of spiritual understanding. For example, just before the miracle of the loaves and fishes, Jesus tested Philip's faith. Jesus asked Philip where they might be able to buy enough food to feed the enormous crowd. Philip, wrapped up in being rational, expressed doubt, fretting that 200 days of work would not raise enough money to feed such a crowd. He seemed to lack the mystical instinct to trust Jesus in handling the overwhelming situation.

In another instance, Philip seemed to be pulled towards reason rather than divine trust. During the Last Supper, Jesus was trying to explain his unity with God, the Father, and how they were one. However, Philip, feeling confused, asked Jesus to show them the Father. Philip evidently desired or needed more definite proof in order to understand and accept what Jesus was saying.

The last mention of Philip the Apostle is in the Acts of the Apostles as having been in the Upper Room prior to the descent of the Holy Spirit. Evidently, although he had a difficult time grasping some spiritual matters, his devotion to Jesus still stood firm.

Philip the Apostle is often confused with another Philip — Philip the Deacon, whose narratives are found within the Acts of the Apostles. Although some early Church fathers believed them to be the same, it is now believed that they were separate persons. Philip the Apostle is believed to have preached the Gospel in Phrygia and was possibly martyred in Hierapolis. However, the place and date of his death are uncertain.

Lk. 6:14 • Jn. 1:43-46 • Jn. 6:5-7
Jn. 12:20-23 • Jn. 14:8-9

ST. MATTHIAS THE APOSTLE

May 14
Patron of Alcoholism Sufferers,
Tailors, Carpenters

And they cast lots for them, and the lot fell on Matthias; and he was enrolled with the eleven apostles.

— ACTS 1:26

The betrayal and death of Judas caused severe disappointment and hurt to the apostles, leaving an uncomfortable void. Recalling a prophecy from the Book of Psalms, "May another take his office," Peter felt a strong compulsion to replace the lost apostle and thereby restore the number of apostles to twelve.

It was during the days of waiting, between Jesus's ascension and the descent of the Holy Spirit, that Peter spoke to a group of about 120 disciples in Jerusalem, sharing his thoughts on the need to replace Judas with someone who knew Jesus well — someone who was an active and committed disciple all the way from the time of Jesus's baptism until His ascension into heaven.

This group of first Christians carefully pondered the situation and suggested two names: Joseph Barsabbas and Matthias. They prayed intensely for heavenly guidance, then proceeded to utilize an ancient Jewish practice, a custom believed to reveal the authentic desire of God — "drawing lots." One common way of drawing lots at that time was to write the name of each candidate on stones and put the stones into a container. Someone would shake the container until one of the stones flew out, signifying the newly "elected." It was probably through this particular system of "drawing lots" that Matthias became the replacement for Judas.

Unfortunately, very little was written about Matthias in the Bible. However, a few intriguing details — some conflicting — were written down by early Church historians. For example, it was recorded that Matthias was a popular preacher on the rejection of earthly desires. He supposedly spent much time stressing the impossibility of serving both God and pleasure. Tradition has Matthias preaching the Gospel in several different locations; however, most sources wrote of him preaching in Judea, where most believe he was ultimately stoned to death.

Acts 1:15-26 • Ps. 69:26 • Ps. 109:8 • Lk. 22:30

ST. BARNABAS

June 11
Patron of Peacemaking;
Protection from Hailstorms

Thus Joseph who was surnamed by the apostles Barnabas (which means, Son of encouragement), a Levite, a native of Cyprus, sold a field which belonged to him, and brought the money and laid it at the apostles' feet.

— ACTS 4:36-37

Although Barnabas does not stand out like many other individuals in the Bible, he actually had a profound effect on the development of Christianity. Barnabas's actual name was Joseph, but evidently he was blessed with a positive demeanor — the apostles decided to call him Barnabas, which means "son of encouragement."

Barnabas was actually the first believer in Jerusalem to welcome the once terrifying Saul (later to be known as Paul). He felt convinced that Saul had had a true conversion and that his vicious persecutions had ended. Saul may never have been accepted by the apostles if it were not for Barnabas.

Barnabas greatly impacted making the new faith universal, or "catholic." The earliest followers were predominantly Jewish. They considered their belief in Christ to be an extension of Judaism, that Jesus had come for Jews alone, and that Gentiles were more or less left out of the picture. When word got to Jerusalem that some Greek Gentiles in Antioch were being taught about Jesus, they decided to send over their "son of encouragement," Barnabas, to investigate.

When Barnabas arrived in Antioch, he was overjoyed at the grace of God he found in the hearts of these Gentiles. It was at this point that Barnabas began to understand that Jesus had come for all, not just for Jews. He heartily encouraged these Gentiles to continue their devotion to Christ. Saul soon joined Barnabas in Antioch, where the two men spent a year working with these inspiring Gentile converts. It was during this time that the term "Christian" began to be used.

Later on, Barnabas traveled with Paul on his first missionary journey and attended the Council of Jerusalem. There, he encouraged the early Church leaders to relax the strict Mosaic Law for the many devoted Gentile converts. Soon after, Barnabas journeyed with his cousin, John Mark (author of the second Gospel), to Cyprus for more evangelizing.

Although Barnabas is rarely mentioned after this, there is no doubt that his acts of "encouragement" continued, having a perpetual and favorable impact upon Christianity.

Acts 9:26-27 • Acts 11:20-26 • Acts 12:25-15:41 • Col. 4:10

ST. JOHN THE BAPTIST

June 24
Patron of Baptism, Converts,
Convulsion Sufferers

"And why is this granted to me, that the mother of my Lord should come to me? For behold, when the voice of your greeting came to my ears, the child in my womb leaped for joy."

— LK. 1:43-44

John the Baptist possessed a keenly spiritual intuition all the way from the time in his mother's womb until his death. As a young adult, John spent years in the wilderness near the Jordan River, fasting and praying, preparing his soul to grasp the mystical event soon to take place: the coming of the Lord. He knew many other people needed to prepare their souls as well, so John began to preach to and encourage people, baptizing anyone who desired it with water from the Jordan.

Countless people felt compelled to go to listen to and contemplate the things John had to say: repentance, love for others, and respect for all. Some people were ill at ease with what he had to say; the challenge was too uncomfortable. Others were thunderstruck. They eagerly changed their lifestyles, undergoing baptism as a symbol of their renewed lives.

When Jesus arrived one day requesting baptism, John was stunned and protested his unworthiness. He knew Jesus was the one everyone waited for — the Messiah, the divine Savior.

Only after Jesus assured him that the baptism was necessary did John perform the task, probably with great awe.

John's preaching of moral living eventually brought about his own death. The tetrarch Herod Antipas had taken the wife of his stepbrother as his own and was offended by John's charge of wrongdoing. But, although Antipas was indignant with John, he had a certain respect for him as well; instead of having John killed, he merely threw him in prison.

Then one night, at a banquet with many friends, Herod Antipas's stepdaughter danced for him and his guests; she so delighted them all that the king offered to grant her any wish. When Salome — urged on by her mother — requested John the Baptist's head on a platter, the king immediately regretted making the very public promise. But, under compulsion to keep his word, Antipas reluctantly ordered the cruel deed to be done.

Lk. 1:10-17 · Lk. 1:57-66 · Lk. 1:80 · Mk. 1:2-8
Mt. 3:13-14 · Jn. 3:22-30

ST. PAUL

June 29
Patron of Writers, Musicians,
Lay People

"And I fell to the ground and heard a voice saying to me, 'Saul, Saul, why do you persecute me?' And I answered, 'Who are you, Lord?' And he said to me, 'I am Jesus of Nazareth whom you are persecuting.'"

— ACTS 22:7-8

Paul (also known as Saul) is a phenomenal character from the Bible who went from being one of the most violent tormenters of Christians to one of their most zealous supporters.

Saul had been a devout Jew with a fierce commitment to Old Testament Scriptures. As the early Christians began to take root and grow, he felt threatened and sought ways to squash this new faith. He witnessed the deadly stoning of an assistant to the apostles (Stephen), and with great determination hunted down and persecuted countless other Christians. He was actually in the process of searching out more believers of Christ to terrorize when his destructive zeal came to a screeching halt.

As Saul was on the way to Damascus, a brilliant flash of light suddenly burst about him, causing him to fall to the ground. Lying there stunned, he heard a voice. It was Jesus, from heaven, questioning Paul's persecutions. An astounded Saul pulled himself up and realized he was blind. His traveling companions had to guide him the rest of the way to Damascus. After three days, a man named Ananias, directed by a vision, sought out Saul and healed him of his blindness through the power of the Holy Spirit, and Saul immediately requested baptism.

This 180-degree turn was a perfect boost for the new faith. Saul's vehement loathing turned to undaunted love and support. Soon to be referred to as "Paul," this great Christian began to preach wherever he could; when he couldn't preach, he wrote letters. His words, both verbal and written, struck a responsive chord in innumerable people's hearts and influenced multitudes who joyously came to believe in and love Jesus. However, Paul's embracing of the Faith brought him persecution in turn — beatings, riots, and imprisonments. Nevertheless, his preachings and letters have had a wondrous and powerful ripple effect on Christianity even to this day.

Tradition tells us that Emperor Nero had Paul beheaded. It is believed that the site of his burial is where the beautiful church of St. Paul Outside The Walls in Rome now stands, a perfect testimony to Paul's tremendous gifts to Christianity.

Acts 8:1-3 · Acts 9:1-30 · Acts 16:1-40
Acts 28:15-16, 30-31 · 2 Tim. 4:7

ST. PETER THE APOSTLE

June 29
Patron of Fishermen, Calmness, Clockmakers

"And I tell you, you are Peter, and on this rock I will build my Church, and the gates of Hades shall not prevail against it. I will give you the keys of the kingdom of heaven."

— MT. 16:18-19B

According to Luke's Gospel, Peter's calling to apostleship occurred one morning after a long night of unsuccessful fishing. While Peter was cleaning his net, Jesus came along and encouraged him to lower the net into some deep water. Peter skeptically complied — and the net became filled with an unmanageable amount of fish. Peter's heart was immediately overwhelmed; his tentative belief in Jesus solidified, and Jesus commanded Peter to follow Him.

Peter's behavior appears outspoken (he has far more quotes in the Gospels than any other apostle), inquisitive, and fervent. He had a keen desire to follow Jesus wholeheartedly, yet his faith would sometimes waver. For example, at the Last Supper, Jesus predicted that Peter would one day deny him three times before a cock crowed. Peter was aghast and unbelieving until this bitter event did occur, during the sham trial of Jesus. We're told that Peter became inconsolable as the prophesied crowing reached his ears.

When Mary Magdalene announced to Peter that Jesus had resurrected, he could not believe her. However, even

41

with his doubts, Peter ran to the tomb. He was astonished as he viewed the emptiness. Shortly after, Jesus appeared to Peter and a few other disciples and assigned Peter the chore of "feeding his sheep."

At Pentecost, Peter and the other disciples became filled with the Holy Spirit and inexplicably began speaking in foreign tongues. When people nearby heard the unlikely voices and words, they accused the disciples of having had too much wine. This accusation prompted Peter to deliver a profound speech, referencing Scripture, that gave support to Jesus being the Messiah. His sermon was so compelling that some 3,000 people were baptized that day.

From then on, Peter led the Church with great conviction. His works were inspired, intense, and miraculous. He traveled to different places, dealing with both enthusiastic converts and hostile persecution, and ultimately settled in Rome. It was there that Peter eventually was crucified (some say upside down), during the persecution of Emperor Nero in the mid-60s A.D.

Lk. 5:1-11 · Mt. 4:18-22 · Jn. 1:35-42 · Mk. 14:27-31
Mk. 14:66-72 · Acts 3:1-10

ST. THOMAS THE APOSTLE

July 3
Patron of Architects

Thomas answered him, "My Lord and my God!"

— Jn. 20:28

Although there are countless stories of doubt in the Bible, it is Thomas's incident that seems to catch the most attention, earning him the nickname of "Doubting Thomas." Fortunately, John's Gospel and some early Church historians give additional information on Thomas, helping searchers to realize that the doubting story was only one part of Thomas's experience as an apostle.

John's first account of Thomas actually displays a man of tremendous faith. Jesus had barely escaped a fierce stoning in Jerusalem when, just a few days later, he received word that his friend Lazarus was quite ill. Lazarus lived in Bethany, a very short distance from Jerusalem, and Jesus felt strongly compelled to go there, knowing that a miracle surrounding Lazarus's death was necessary to illustrate the glory of God. However, the apostles were aghast and tried to discourage Jesus from returning to an area where he had so recently been almost killed. Ironically, it was Thomas who was the believing one. He bravely encouraged all to go to Bethany with Jesus, even if it meant death.

Thomas's "doubting" story took place after Jesus's resurrection. When Jesus appeared to the disciples in all His glory, for some reason Thomas was absent. Later, when Thomas rejoined the disciples, they told him all that had happened, but he was unconvinced. He then made his famous statement about needing to place his finger and hand in Jesus's wounds before he would believe. A week later, Jesus again appeared, and this time Thomas was there. Jesus gently invited Thomas to touch His wounds, and Thomas then exclaimed his ardent belief in the risen Jesus.

Most Tradition points to Thomas as having evangelized in India following Pentecost. Today, there is a devout community of Catholics on the Malabar Coast of India who call themselves the "Christians of St. Thomas." They claim that their community began through the teachings of Thomas himself, and research shows ample evidence that this Christian community indeed has very ancient roots.

It is believed that Thomas was speared to death for his works in India. Tradition tells that he was initially buried in India, but that over time, many of his remains were transferred to Mesopotamia, and then to Ortona, Italy.

Jn. 11:8, 16 • Jn. 14:5-7
Jn. 20:24-29 • Jn. 21:2-14 • Acts 1:13

STS. AQUILA AND PRISCILLA

July 8
Patrons of Married Couples

After this he left Athens and went to Corinth. And he found a Jew named Aquila, a native of Pontus, lately come from Italy with his wife Priscilla.

— ACTS 18:1-2A

We first meet the married couple Aquila and Priscilla (also known as Prisca) in Corinth, when their path providentially crossed with Paul's. Paul had just left Athens in the midst of his second missionary journey, while Aquila and Priscilla had left Rome due to an eviction of Jews by Emperor Claudius. This wonderful chance meeting gave a great lift to Paul's works. This married couple gave Paul rest and refuge at their home; Paul gave Aquila and Priscilla divinely inspired spiritual guidance.

When Paul was done with his work in Corinth, he, Aquila, and Priscilla set sail. They made a stop at Ephesus, where the devout couple decided to stay. Many Ephesians had heard Paul's wonderful preaching and wanted him to stay as well; however, he felt compelled to move on to Syria. Perhaps Paul's decision to leave Ephesus behind was based on his confidence in Aquila and Priscilla to effectively advocate the truths of Jesus Christ.

Aquila and Pricilla were indeed valuable evangelizers in Ephesus. They let their house there be used as a place of worship, and worked hard to teach the Ephesians of the glory of Christ. One day, they came across a phenomenal speaker named Apollos. Apollos had a great understanding of the Old Testament Scriptures, and when he learned of Jesus, he had no doubt that Jesus was the promised Messiah. He used his preaching skills to share this marvelous news. Aquila and Priscilla, hearing some of his preaching, realized that although his desires were ardent and fervent, he was missing some key points. They wasted no time helping Apollos refine his knowledge and enable him to preach more exactly, which he did . . . in Ephesus and beyond.

In a letter to the Romans, Paul expressed appreciation to Aquila and Priscilla, mentioning how they had once "risked their necks" for him. Although the specifics of the story are never mentioned, the comment illustrates their devotion to Paul's work.

There is very little else written about this wonderful married couple after the New Testament writings. Some Church historians wrote that they were eventually martyred for their works of faith while in Rome.

Acts 18:1-3 • Acts 18:18-19 • Acts 18:24-26 • Rom. 16:3

JASON

July 12
Patron of Guest Keepers

And when they could not find them [Paul and Silas], they dragged Jason and some of the brethren before the city authorities, crying, "These men who have turned the world upside down have come here also."

— ACTS 17:6

Jason must have been aware of the many people in his hometown of Thessalonica who feared and despised the numerous Christians spreading throughout the city. However, the risk of ostracism didn't threaten Jason; his heart was unconditionally open to truth, and he felt an intense tug to follow the teachings of Jesus. Jason bravely allowed the Christian leaders Paul and Silas to stay at his home while they were preaching in Thessalonica, hoping to support their works by giving them a place to rest.

It was during his second great missionary journey that Paul stayed at Jason's house. While there, Paul spent three Sabbaths at the synagogue discussing Scriptures with other worshippers, presenting clear connections between Old Testament Scriptures and the divinity of Jesus. While many Thessalonians in the synagogue were convinced and welcomed Christianity with joy, others became annoyed and aggravated.

A few intimidated citizens pulled together a hapless group of men found loitering in the public square and riled them up. This outlandish group marched to Jason's house, hoping to find Paul and Silas. Because Paul and Silas were not there, they grabbed Jason and some others instead and brought them before city officials, intending to scare Jason and his fellow brethren and end Christian influence in Thessalonica. The aggressors' publicly expressed outrage over Jason having claimed that Jesus was a king worked to influence the magistrates . . . somewhat. Jason and his friends were fined and then allowed to go home. Ultimately, however, many Thessalonians welcomed Jesus into their hearts.

Jason is said to have become bishop of Tarsus and then to have died on the Greek island of Corfu. Now, thanks to Jason having opened his home to Paul and Silas, many people in present-day Thessaloniki (Greece) have great devotion to Christ. A popular stop for tourists visiting Thessaloniki is the "House of Jason," a monastery at the believed site of Jason's house. In Corfu, there is a church named after Jason, to help people remember this brave embracer of the Faith.

Acts 17:5-9 • Rom. 16:21

ST. SILAS

July 13
Patron of Assistants

But about midnight Paul and Silas were praying and singing hymns to God, and the prisoners were listening to them, and suddenly there was a great earthquake, so that the foundations of the prison were shaken; and immediately all the doors were opened and every one's chains were unfastened.

— ACTS 16:25-26

While sharing news from the Council of Jerusalem to believers in Antioch, Silas (also known as Silvanus) proved himself to be filled with faith and zeal. Not long after, Paul brought him along as an assistant on his second missionary journey. Silas encountered many adventures while traveling with Paul; however, their time in Philippi seems to have been the most remarkable.

While preaching in Philippi, the two brethren came across a slave girl who also happened to be a fortuneteller. After hearing Paul and Silas preach, the girl felt compelled to trail behind them, constantly shouting out to people, "These people are slaves of the Most High God, who proclaim to you a way of salvation." After many days, the shouting irritated Paul. He turned to the slave girl and in the name of Jesus Christ commanded the spirit within her to leave — which it did!

Just as the disruptive shouting stopped, the girl's clairvoyant abilities ceased as well, causing a great loss of income to her owners. These infuriated slaveholders dragged Silas and Paul to the public square, where they were verbally attacked, stripped, beaten, and then thrown into prison.

The two holy men spent that night in prison singing and praying. Suddenly, at about midnight, an earthquake shook so violently that cell doors burst open and prisoners' chains broke free. Over Silas and Paul's shock and amazement, they heard the distressed voice of the jailer, who was ready to take his own life over the fear of losing his prisoners. Silas and Paul compassionately stopped him and offered him hope that prompted the jailer's spirit to brighten. He became hungry for knowledge of Christianity and even brought Silas and Paul to his home that night, so his family could learn more about Jesus as well. The next day, the magistrates found out that Silas and Paul were Roman citizens and granted them a swift release.

Silas continued to help Paul with further travels, writings, and teachings. It is written that he also spent time with Peter, supporting his evangelizing works as well.

Acts 15:22-35 · Acts 15:40 · Acts 16:16-40
Acts 17:10-15 · 1 Pet. 5:12

ST. JOSEPH BARSABBAS

July 20
Patron of Quiet Holiness

"So one of the men who have accompanied us during all the time that the Lord Jesus went in and out among us . . . must become with us a witness to his resurrection." And they put forward two, Joseph called Barsabbas, who was surnamed Justus, and Matthias.

— ACTS 1:21, 22B-23

Although Joseph Barsabbas Justus is mentioned only once in the Bible, there is a strong indication that he was a man very close to Jesus. Shortly before He ascended into heaven, Jesus told His followers to wait in Jerusalem for the promised Holy Spirit. It was during this time of waiting that Joseph Barsabbas comes up in the Bible.

Peter spent some time reflecting and reading Scriptures during this phase of expectation. After contemplating Psalm 109 ("his office let another take"), he felt compelled to make arrangements to find a replacement for the lost apostle, Judas Iscariot. Peter expressed these feelings to a group of about 120 followers who were also in Jerusalem anticipating the arrival of the Holy Spirit.

Peter laid out guidelines for the replacement apostle. He stated that the new apostle must have been an active follower from the time of Jesus's baptism until the day He ascended into heaven. Because Joseph Barsabbas was one of two men recommended as suitable candidates, Peter's standards make it clear that Joseph Barsabbas must have spent much time with the apostles and witnessed many of the wondrous events in the life of Jesus. He must have known Jesus well and embraced all that He taught. Most historians agree that Joseph Barsabbas was probably one of the "seventy-two" disciples mentioned in Luke's Gospel.

The disciples used a system of "lots" to select the new apostle. The Hebrew meaning of the word "lots" is "destiny." The Jewish people firmly believed that using this technique of possibility, combined with prayer, would reveal the true will of God. It was the second candidate, Matthias, who won the right to apostleship through casting lots. God evidently decided to give Joseph Barsabbas a quieter and less prominent job to do.

Very little is known about Joseph Barsabbas outside of the apostle selection story. One vague legend tells of Joseph drinking some poison without being harmed. It is also written that he was once imprisoned by Emperor Nero for his religious actions, then later released.

Acts 1:15-26 • Ps. 109:8 • Prov. 16:33 • Lk. 10:1-11

ST. MARY MAGDALENE

July 22
Patroness of Penitent Sinners, Contemplative Life

Jesus said to her, "Woman, why are you weeping? Whom do you seek?" Supposing him to be the gardener, she said to him, "Sir, if you have carried him away, tell me where you have laid him, and I will take him away." Jesus said to her, "Mary." She turned and said to him in Hebrew, "Rabboni!" (which means Teacher).

— JN. 20:15-16

A group of women from the region of Galilee had melded together as special followers of Jesus. They apparently traveled with Jesus whenever possible to learn from Him and help minister to His needs. It is from this group that Mary Magdalene, a woman who had previously been possessed by seven demons, emerged.

Most accounts of Mary Magdalene in the Bible take place during the Crucifixion, burial, and resurrection of Jesus. After watching the ghastly horror of Jesus's Crucifixion, Mary Magdalene and some of her Galilean friends brought anointing oils to His burial place. However, because Jesus's death occurred late on a Friday, the anointing had to wait until the end of Sabbath. They watched sadly as Joseph of Arimathea carefully secured Jesus's dead body in a tomb.

Mary Magdalene (again, probably with some friends) went to Jesus's tomb as early as possible the morning after

Sabbath, hoping to take care of the anointing. As she entered the tomb, she was taken aback: Jesus was gone! Overwhelmed and trembling, Mary Magdalene hurried off to tell Peter and the others.

Peter and John, although incredulous at Mary's news, rushed to the tomb. They were also staggered to see it empty. Bewildered, the apostles returned to their homes in a daze while Mary remained at the tomb, weeping with uncontrollable grief. Jesus then appeared and asked Mary why she was crying. Confused and distraught, she did not immediately recognize Jesus until He called her by name. At that moment, Mary Magdalene clearly understood it was her Lord and joyfully reached to embrace Him.

What happened to Mary Magdalene afterwards is hard to verify. Eastern Tradition places her in Ephesus following Pentecost, while other legends claim that Mary traveled to France and became a contemplative. Many believe that her remains have been kept in a monastery in the town of St. Maximin, France, for centuries.

Lk. 8:1-3 • Mt. 27:55-56 • Mk. 15:47-16:8
Lk. 24:1-12 • Jn. 20:11-18

THE THREE WISE MEN

July 24
(Formerly July 23)
Patrons of Traveling, Fever Sufferers;
Against Sudden Death

*When they saw the star, they rejoiced exceedingly with great joy;
and going into the house they saw the child with Mary his mother,
and they fell down and worshiped him. Then, opening their trea-
sures, they offered him gifts, gold, frankincense and myrrh.*

— Mt. 2:10-11

The Magi truly were "wise men" in their genuine desire to
seek out truth and goodness. They evidently had searched
for life's meaning in the skies and discovered a star that led
them to believe that a supreme new king had been born.
Thus, full of faith, they began their long journey from points
east towards Judea.

After traveling great distances, the Magi stopped in Jerusalem. King Herod heard about these curious mystics and
met with them to hear their story. When informed by his
chief priest and scribes that Bethlehem would be the place
of the newborn king, Herod sent the Magi there, requesting
that they return with details on the specific whereabouts of
the baby. He let the Magi think that he was interested in pay-
ing homage to the king himself; secretly, however, he wanted
to plan the death of this infant who threatened his sense of
power.

As the Magi approached Bethlehem, the star seemed to settle over one spot. They approached the place and found the child king of the Jews. These truth-seeking Gentiles fell face down, clearly understanding they were before Someone of greatness, even though His surroundings were meek. They presented to Him gifts of gold, frankincense, and myrrh — exquisite offerings that symbolized kingship, divinity, and death. Although the actual number of the Magi was never recorded, these three gifts have encouraged historians to suggest that there were three.

Before the Magi left Bethlehem, they were warned in a dream of Herod's murderous plan and returned to their homes by a route far from Herod's path. Their brief time with Jesus was truly profound — it signified an invitation for Gentiles to God through Jesus.

A few centuries later, St. Helena discovered the remains of the Magi. They were ultimately transferred to Cologne, Germany, where they are now beautifully entombed on an altar. For many years, it was a tradition for German kings to make a pilgrimage to the altar of the Magi following their coronations.

Mt. 2:1-12 · Mt. 2:16a · Ps. 72:10-11 · Is. 60:6

ST. JAMES THE GREATER

July 25
Patron of Spain, Arthritics,
Soldiers, Pharmacists

And going on from there he saw two other brothers, James the son of Zebedee and John his brother, in the boat with Zebedee their father, mending their nets, and he called them. Immediately they left their boat and their father, and followed him.

— MT. 4:21-22

James the Greater (who was likely older or bigger than James the Less) was a fisherman from Galilee whom Jesus called to be an apostle. This James happened to be a part of a trio of apostles who were with Jesus during three particular occasions. James, his brother John, and Peter made up this distinctive group.

The first James-John-Peter event was the raising of the twelve-year-old daughter of Jairus, a synagogue official who sought out Jesus for her healing. Jesus went to the man's house and brought Jairus, his wife, and the three apostles into the girl's room with Him. Then He commanded the dead girl to rise and, miraculously, she got up and began to walk about.

The second unique experience was Jesus's Transfiguration. Jesus again had His three closest apostles — James, John, and Peter — with Him on a mountaintop when His body became luminous. He was joined by Moses and Elijah, who appeared with Him in glory.

The third episode that the threesome shared with Jesus was His agony at Gethsemane. Jesus brought all His apostles to Gethsemane, but invited only James, John, and Peter closest to His actual place of prayer. He shared with only these three His troubled heart and asked them to keep watch.

James the Greater and his brother, John, shared a unique nickname given to them by Jesus: *Boanerges,* Aramaic for "Sons of Thunder." Most Biblical historians attribute this nickname to an event that took place in Samaria. Some Samaritans had refused to open their ears and hearts to messages of Jesus, so James and John asked Jesus for permission to call fire down from heaven upon the town.

From Pentecost until his beheading in Jerusalem around A.D. 42, James's whereabouts are unclear. Enduring legends suggest that he spent that time frame preaching in Spain. Additional accounts assert that at some point following his death, his remains were miraculously transported to Spain, where they were ultimately entombed within a beautiful cathedral. Now each year, thousands of pilgrims hike to this holy site, Santiago de Compostela, for spiritual renewal.

Lk. 8:51 • Lk. 9:28-31 • Mt. 26:36-38 • Mk. 3:17
Lk. 9:54 • Acts 12:2

ST. LAZARUS

July 29
(Formerly December 17)
Patron of Emergency Medical Technicians

When he had said this, he cried with a loud voice, "Lazarus, come out." The dead man came out, his hands and feet bound with bandages, and his face wrapped with a cloth. Jesus said to them, "Unbind him, and let him go."

— Jn. 11:43-44

Lazarus and his two sisters, Martha and Mary, lived in Bethany, a town just a few miles from Jerusalem. These three siblings were good friends with Jesus, so when Lazarus became terribly ill, Martha and Mary sent word to Jesus letting Him know of their brother's condition. The sisters desperately hoped that He would visit and restore the health of their brother.

When Jesus received the sisters' message, He understood that Lazarus's dreadful condition was a part of God's plan — that the events that were to surround Lazarus within the days to come would beautifully demonstrate the glory of God and help people to better understand who Jesus was. After deliberately waiting a few days, Jesus set out to Bethany.

By the time Jesus arrived, Lazarus had been dead for four days. Martha and Mary were terribly distressed by Jesus's coming too late to help their brother. But when Jesus asked that the stone before Lazarus's tomb be pushed aside, as anguished — and bewildered — as the onlookers had to have been, they did as He asked.

Before a gathered crowd, Jesus spoke out to God in prayer and then forcefully exclaimed, "Lazarus, come out!" Before the eyes of all, Lazarus rose up and stepped outside the tomb, still wrapped in his burial bands, and Jesus directed the awestruck crowd to untie the burial wrappings and let him go.

News of this miracle spread rapidly, creating a significant turning point in Jesus's ministry and life. Many people went from mere curiosity or indifference to following Him wholeheartedly. This shift in public attitude infuriated the already upset synagogue authorities. They began to make plans for the death of Jesus and even thought about eliminating Lazarus along with Him.

But, although the Sanhedrin succeeded in having Jesus crucified, Lazarus was spared. After Pentecost, he is said to have preached in Cyprus for many years. His relics were reportedly discovered there in 899 and transferred to Constantinople; from there, they were moved to Autun, France, where they are now venerated at the Cathedral of St. Lazarus.

Jn. 11:1-44 · Jn. 12:1-2 · Jn. 12:9-11 · Lk. 10:38-42

ST. MARTHA

July 29
Patroness of Homemakers, Servants, Unmarried Women

She said to him, "Yes, Lord; I believe that you are the Christ, the Son of God, he who is coming into the world."

— Jn. 11:27

Martha, her brother Lazarus, and her sister Mary shared a home in Bethany, a few miles from Jerusalem. Martha appears to have been the organizer of the siblings' home, a person with a very strong sense of responsibility. On one occasion when Jesus visited, Martha's sister Mary stopped doing any work in order to spend time with Him. Martha scurried about, feeling resentful as she did the household chores for both women. Finally, she couldn't take any more and asked Jesus to tell Mary to help her. Instead, He encouraged Martha to let go of her housework for awhile in order to spend time working on spiritual matters instead.

Another profound story including Martha centers on her brother's death. When Lazarus became gravely ill, Martha sent word to Jesus requesting Him to come to Bethany, but Lazarus died before Jesus arrived. Nevertheless, when word reached Martha that Jesus was finally approaching the village, she rushed out to greet Him, her joy at seeing her Lord mingled with grief. She became further confused when Jesus asked for the stone before Lazarus's tomb to be pushed away.

When Jesus had arrived too late to save her brother, Martha had already resigned herself to Lazarus's death and put all her hopes into her brother rising on the last day — so why, she asked, open the tomb and expose his decaying body? She didn't imagine the possibility that Jesus could raise Lazarus back to life *then and there*. But as she watched Jesus command her brother to rise, her faith took on dramatic new strength and depth.

Martha served dinner for the Lord again just six days before Passover, an occasion on which people curious to see Jesus and the revived Lazarus gathered nearby.

St. Martha can help us to consider the need and difficulty of balancing our everyday and spiritual lives.

Lk. 10:38-42 • Jn. 11:1-44 • Jn. 12:1-11

ST. BARTHOLOMEW
THE APOSTLE

August 24
Patron of Butchers, Leatherworkers, Calmness

Nathanael [Bartholomew] said to him, "How do you know me?"
Jesus answered him, "Before Philip called you, when you were
under the fig tree, I saw you." Nathanael answered him, "Rabbi,
you are the Son of God! You are the King of Israel!"

— JN. 1:48-49

The name *Bartholomew* has Aramaic roots and means "Son of Tolmai." Because he is usually considered to be the same as the Nathanael in John's Gospel, many believe that Bartholomew's full name was probably Nathanael Bartholomew.

Nathanael Bartholomew's introduction in John's Gospel is very intriguing. His close friend, Philip, had just met Jesus and was struck with Jesus's mysticism and goodness. Philip had complete confidence that Jesus was the Messiah. He ran to tell Bartholomew — but Bartholomew, evidently a bit prejudiced, found it unbelievable that anyone of importance could come from Nazareth.

However, when Bartholomew came face to face with Jesus himself, his heart quickly changed. Jesus's first words about Bartholomew were peculiar: He called Bartholomew a "true Israelite with no guile." Bartholomew's nature evidently was clear and easy to read, lacking pretense and deceit. He spoke his true feelings.

Bartholomew then asked Jesus how He knew him. When Jesus replied that He had seen Bartholomew under a fig tree one day, Bartholomew's whole countenance transformed. Jesus's being from Nazareth no longer mattered; Bartholomew was ready to profess that Jesus was indeed the Son of God and the King of Israel.

There are no specific stories on Bartholomew outside of John's "calling" story. However, because he was an apostle, we know that Bartholomew spent a great deal of time with Jesus, learning from Him and experiencing many wondrous and miraculous events. He was blessed to have witnessed the risen Christ and encounter the coming of the Holy Spirit. Because he was selected as an apostle, Bartholomew had the authority to preach, cure people, and drive out demons.

Legends state that Bartholomew traveled to India, Armenia, Ethiopia, and Persia after Pentecost. Ancient historians wrote that he lived an austere, yet happy life. It is believed that he was flayed alive in India.

Most of his relics are believed to be entombed within the church of St. Bartholomew on Tiber Island in the Tiber River in Rome.

Mt. 10:3 · Lk. 6:14 · Acts 1:13 · Jn. 1:45-49 · Jn. 21:2-3

ST. JOSEPH OF ARIMATHEA

August 31
(Formerly March 17)
Patron of Undertakers, Pallbearers

*And when evening had come, since it was the day of Prepara-
tion, that is, the day before the sabbath, Joseph of Arimathea, a
respected member of the council, who was also himself looking for
the kingdom of God, took courage and went to Pilate, and asked
for the body of Jesus.*

— MK. 15:42-43

Rich, distinguished, courageous, virtuous, and righteous
are words used in the Gospels to describe Joseph of Arimathea. Remarkably, Joseph was a member of the Sanhedrin,
the council that condemned Jesus to death. However, Joseph
lived the way a Sanhedrin member was supposed to, as an
earnest seeker of truth. He was opposed to Jesus's crucifixion
sentence because his genuine search for truth had brought
him to believe in all Jesus stood for. Joseph feared ostracism
from his fellow Jews, however — so initially, he kept his following of Jesus a secret.

Upon the death of Jesus, Joseph of Arimathea found the
courage to make the official request to take away the dead
body. Normally, crucified bodies were left for vultures to
devour, and approaching Pontius Pilate to request permission
on this matter must have been difficult — Joseph must have
known that it would likely compromise any worldly respect

that he had. Maybe he couldn't bear the thought of Jesus suffering even more degradation; maybe that's what prompted Joseph to realize that he had to risk revealing his secret.

Jesus's death occurred on a Friday afternoon, making Sabbath just a few hours away. Joseph enlisted help from a man named Nicodemus to quickly tend to the basic needs of the burial. Fortunately, he actually had a tomb already prepared, recently cut out of some nearby limestone. (Some historians suggest that it might well have been prepared for Joseph himself.) So, rather than hastily tossing the body of Jesus into a common grave, Joseph carefully wrapped the body in a linen shroud and reverently placed it into this clean tomb.

Although there is no further mention of him in the Bible, through these few recorded acts, St. Joseph of Arimathea offers inspiration and encouragement to step out of our "comfort zones" in order to do the will of God.

Mt. 27:57-60 • Mk. 15:42-46 • Lk. 23:50-53 • Jn. 19:38-42

ST. PHOEBE

September 3
Patroness of Women's Ministries

I commend to you our sister Phoebe, a deaconess of the Church at Cenchreae, that you may receive her in the Lord as befits the saints, and help her in whatever she may require from you, for she has been a helper of many and of myself as well.

— ROM. 16:1-2

The only reference to Phoebe in the Bible occurs in the last chapter of Paul's letter to the Romans. Many claim that the words surrounding Phoebe's name strongly suggest that it was Phoebe herself who actually delivered that letter; in any event, although the mention is brief, we can infer much from it.

His written introduction of Phoebe to the Romans is intriguing to ponder. It is full of warmth and praise, encouraging a wonderful, accepting, and generous welcome, as if she were a holy one (a "saint").

Because she was from the church in Cenchreae (a port in Greece, a few miles from Corinth), it becomes very plausible that she was Greek. Her ability and willingness to travel all the way from Cenchreae to Rome shows that she had an outstanding belief in the ways of Christ. Such a long and arduous journey had to have been made by someone open to adventure and deeply committed to the mission.

Phoebe is mentioned as being a "deaconess" (in some translations, a "minister"). The duties of a deaconess or minister at that time in Church history are not clear, but it's safe to assume that the role entailed generous involvement and support one way or another.

One can imagine some possibilities in Phoebe's case. No husband is mentioned, so perhaps she was unmarried and had the time to devote herself to the needs of the early Church. Perhaps she had great talent in effectively conveying the great truths of Christianity. Perhaps she had the financial means to give monetary assistance. Perhaps she offered her home as a place of worship.

Phoebe is an excellent example of how women have crucial roles in the Church. Whatever talents they have, there is a way to bring them to the altar.

Rom. 16:1-2 • Acts 18:18b • Phil. 1:1 • 1 Tim. 3:8-13

ST. MATTHEW THE APOSTLE

September 21
Patron of Bankers, Accountants

As Jesus passed on from there, he saw a man called Matthew sitting at the tax office; and he said to him, "Follow me." And he rose and followed him.

— Mt. 9:9

Matthew (also known as Levi in the Gospels of Luke and Mark) was a Jewish tax collector, or publican, living in Capernaum. Tax collectors at that time were known as dishonest and corrupt people who would take advantage of anyone they could, overtaxing as much as possible for personal gain. So, although Matthew most likely lived in comfort, he would have also experienced much ostracism from his fellow Jews.

When Jesus called Matthew to apostleship, his sudden acceptance is striking to imagine. All three Gospel accounts state that he immediately got up and followed Jesus. Luke emphasized how Matthew left everything he had behind in order to go with Jesus. It would be much easier to suppose that such a sinful and hated Jew would hesitate, either feeling unworthy or considering such a dramatic life change to be too daunting.

Another interesting point to notice in Matthew's calling is the illustration of Jesus associating with sinners. After his drastic transformation, Matthew threw a big feast for Jesus and invited many of his tax-collector-type friends. The Pharisees and scribes had a hard time accepting Jesus mixing with such deplorable people. The Lord's words must have stung as He compared himself to a physician whose duty required healing the sick rather than the healthy.

Tradition has named Matthew as the author of the first Gospel. This particular Gospel was written for Jews who chose to embrace Christianity, clearly showing the countless fulfillments of Old Testament prophecies that came to pass through the life of Jesus.

It is unknown what happened to Matthew after Pentecost. Because he was never mentioned in any of Paul's epistles, it is assumed by many that he did not travel within the Mediterranean region. Tradition holds that he preached in Persia, likely died of old age, and that his remains were transferred to Salerno, Italy, where they are now kept within the city's cathedral.

Mt. 9:9-13 • Mk. 2:13-17 • Lk. 5:27-32
Mt. 10:3 • Acts 1:13

ST. ELIZABETH

September 23
(Formerly November 5)
Patroness of Expectant Mothers

And when Elizabeth heard the greeting of Mary, the child leaped in her womb; and Elizabeth was filled with the holy Spirit and she exclaimed with a loud cry, "Blessed are you among women, and blessed is the fruit of your womb!"

— Lk. 1:41-42

The heartwarming narratives of Elizabeth can be found in the first chapter of Luke's Gospel. Elizabeth was a good and devout woman who had suffered many years of a sad barrenness. One day, the angel Gabriel appeared to her husband Zechariah and declared that Elizabeth would soon conceive and bear a son of tremendous virtue. Not long after this proclamation, Elizabeth did indeed conceive and quietly kept homebound for five months, praising God for the beautiful gift of new life.

At Elizabeth's sixth month of expectancy, the archangel Gabriel appeared again, this time to Elizabeth's relative Mary. Gabriel announced to Mary the forthcoming birth of Jesus and let her know of Elizabeth's upcoming joy. Mary, full of amazement, journeyed to the hill country of Judea to visit her elderly kinswoman. As Elizabeth heard Mary's greeting, she felt a profound quickening within her womb. She immediately knew from this reaction of her unborn son that she was in the presence of greatness, that Mary's babe was to be a man of vast love and widespread influence. Filled with the Spirit, Elizabeth spoke words that would one day become known as the second line of the beautiful prayer, Hail Mary: "Blessed are you among women, and blessed is the fruit of your womb."

After a three-month-long visit from Mary, Elizabeth gave birth to her son. All neighbors and relatives were delighted over her wondrous blessing. However, they were confused over the chosen name of John, wondering why Elizabeth would not name her son after her husband, Zechariah. Zechariah, who had been struck dumb over his disbelief in Gabriel's earlier announcement, confirmed the name of John by writing on a tablet. At that moment of agreement, he regained his voice. The neighbors were astonished over such extraordinary events surrounding Elizabeth's child.

Elizabeth shares the Sept. 23 feast day with her husband, Zechariah. In addition, Elizabeth shares a feast day with Mary on May 31 to honor the three months of her visitation by Mary.

Lk. 1:5-25 · Lk. 1:39-45 · Lk. 1:57-66 · Lk. 1:80

ST. ZECHARIAH

September 23
(Formerly November 5)
Patron of Fathers-to-Be

But the angel said to him, "Do not be afraid, Zechariah, for your prayer is heard, and your wife Elizabeth will bear you a son, and you shall call his name John. And you will have joy and gladness, and many will rejoice at his birth."

— LK. 1:13-14

Curiously, there are more than thirty Zechariahs in the Old Testament, yet only one in the New Testament. This New Testament Zechariah was recorded by Luke as being a very good and holy man, a priest for the Temple of Jerusalem. Sadly, however, he and his wife Elizabeth had been unable to have any children, causing distress in their lives.

One day Zechariah was in the Temple when a remarkable visitor appeared — the archangel Gabriel, who let Zechariah know that he was to soon become a father. The archangel promised that this long-awaited son would be filled with the Holy Spirit and would inspire the hearts of many. But Zechariah was stunned and incredulous, as he and Elizabeth were both elderly, and asked the angel for a sign. Because of his doubting heart, Zechariah was punished by being made unable to speak. Shortly after this angelic visitation, Elizabeth did in fact conceive and remained in seclusion for the first five months of her pregnancy.

After their baby son was born, Elizabeth announced to jubilant friends and family that they would name their son John. The relatives, taken aback, urged her to name the boy for his father, but the speechless Zechariah took a tablet and wrote, "John is his name." As soon as he showed them this message, his ability to speak was miraculously restored. Zechariah was then filled with the Holy Spirit and exclaimed a heartfelt prayer of blessing to the Lord. This proclamation became known as the "Canticle of Zechariah," or *Benedictus*, which is Latin for "blessed."

These friends and family were astonished over the wonders surrounding John's birth. They quickly shared the glorious news with others in the hill country of Judea. They were convinced that the Lord was with this unique family in an extraordinary way.

Zechariah is not mentioned again in the Bible. He and his wife, Elizabeth, share Sept. 23 as a feast day.

Lk. 1:5-25 · Lk. 1:57-66 · Lk. 1:67-79

ST. GABRIEL THE ARCHANGEL

September 29
Patron of Communication Arts

In the sixth month, the angel Gabriel was sent from God to a city of Galilee called Nazareth, to a virgin betrothed to a man whose name was Joseph, of the house of David; and the virgin's name was Mary. And he came to her and said, "Hail, full of grace, the Lord is with you!"

— LK. 1:26-28

Gabriel is an archangel, a higher-ranking angel devoted to praising and serving God. One particular task of archangels has been to deliver divine messages during certain pivotal times in history, and Gabriel appears with heavenly messages in both the Old and New Testaments.

His name is first mentioned in the book of Daniel. Daniel was a prophet who lived in Babylon (present-day Iraq) while the people of Judah were being held captive there. Gabriel appeared on two different occasions to Daniel, offering him and his countrymen hope, assurance, and strength during their long and difficult internment.

Gabriel is very prominent in the New Testament within the Gospel of Luke as he announces two very significant events. First, he appeared to Zechariah, an elderly priest of the Temple of Jerusalem. While Zechariah was performing a religious obligation of burning incense within the sanctuary of the Lord, Gabriel became visible to him and told Zechariah that he would soon become the father of an exceptional son who would do much to change the hearts of many. The old priest expressed difficulty in believing this proclamation, because he and his wife had never been able to have children and were quite elderly by this time. Because of his doubt, Zechariah was struck dumb until several months later, on the day that his infant son, John (the Baptist), was circumcised.

About six months after his appearance to Zechariah, Gabriel visited Mary, the gentle young woman betrothed to Joseph, and announced to her that she had been chosen to be the mother of God's son! Mary, like Zechariah, expressed doubt upon hearing Gabriel's words, but the archangel offered Mary reassurance, patience, and further explanation. When Mary humbly expressed her desire to do God's will, Gabriel left her presence.

Dan. 8:15-26 · Dan. 9:21-27 · Lk. 1:10-20 · Lk. 1:26-38

ST. MICHAEL THE ARCHANGEL

September 29
Patron of Paratroopers, Artists,
A Holy Death

At that time shall arise Michael, the great prince who has charge of your people. And there shall be a time of trouble, such as never has been since there was a nation till that time; but at that time your people shall be delivered, every one whose name shall be found written in the book.

— DAN. 12:1

The archangel Michael is specifically named in the Bible within three books: Daniel, Jude, and Revelation.

In Daniel, Michael is mentioned on only three different occasions; however the words used to describe him are remarkable. He is referred to as "one of the chief princes," "standing as a reinforcement and a bulwark," and "the great prince who has charge of your people." The book of Daniel clearly portrays Michael as being prepared to fight various evil forces on behalf of the Jewish people. The reference to Michael within the book of Jude is very brief and skims over an event in which Michael quarreled with the devil over the body of Moses. In Revelation, Michael is specifically mentioned one time only — presented as victorious over a brutal dragon during a war taking place in heaven.

These verses, portraying Michael as a powerful leader against malice, have given countless people, both Jewish and

Christian, reason to turn to this archangel for safeguard and protection. They call upon Michael during times of distress and trouble, especially when facing situations that feel evil.

The archangel Michael has manifested himself to many over the centuries. Two locations honoring this heavenly general have become inspirational places of pilgrimage and prayer.

- In the fifth century in Gargano, Italy, St. Michael appeared to a bishop who was in a cave investigating a mystical occurrence surrounding a wandering bull. St. Michael requested a chapel to be built within the cave; the chapel was indeed built, and the cave now is known as Monte Sant'Angelo.

- In 708, Michael appeared to St. Aubert, who at that time was a bishop in France. Michael ordered Aubert to build a chapel on a nearby mountain. Over the years, a monastery and several other buildings have been added to the site. This spot became known as Le Mont-St.-Michel and is a favorite place of pilgrimage in France.

Dan. 10:13 · Dan. 10:21 · Dan. 12:1
Jude 9 · Rev. 12:7-9

ST. RAPHAEL THE ARCHANGEL

September 29
Patron of Young People, Peacefulness, Healing

Raphael said, "Take courage! God has healing in store for you; so take courage!"

— Tob. 5:10 (NAB)

The archangel Raphael is presented within the beautiful story of Tobit — a deuterocanonical book in the Old Testament. In this story, God sent Raphael down to earth to assist two distraught people, Tobit and Sarah.

Tobit was a good and righteous man who had lost his eyesight, causing his small family great anguish. At the same time, about 300 miles away, a distant young relative, Sarah, was also grief-stricken. She had attempted to marry seven different times, but each groom was struck dead by a cruel demon.

In need of some money due to his blindness, Tobit sent his only child, Tobiah, to a distant town to collect funds that he had deposited with a friend. Tobiah found a reliable traveling companion — a man who called himself Azariah, but who was actually the archangel Raphael in disguise.

In the midst of their journey, Tobiah caught an unusual fish. Azariah (Raphael) directed Tobiah to take out the heart, liver, and gall to keep for medicine. Later on as the two travelers neared their destination, the concealed archangel insisted they pay a visit to Sarah's family. Almost instantly, Tobiah fell in love with Sarah. Although he knew the story of her seven dead husbands, he still asked to marry her. Raphael instructed Tobiah to place the fish heart and liver on some embers in the bridal chamber. The odor of the smoldering heart and liver was revolting to the evil spirit; he fled, and Tobiah was spared.

Raphael, still appearing as Azariah, left the newly married couple behind to complete the journey alone. He collected the money, then returned to the house of Sarah's parents. The angel, Tobiah, and Sarah then set off for the long trip back to Tobit's home. When the three arrived, Raphael had Tobiah smear the fish gall into his father's eyes, which miraculously healed Tobit of his blindness.

The successful marriage, along with Tobit's restored eyesight, caused great elation for the two small families. Before returning to God, Raphael revealed his true nature and identity.

Tob. 5:1-8 · Tob. 6:2-6 · Tob. 7:9-11
Tob. 8:1-8 · Tob. 12:15

GUARDIAN ANGELS

October 2
Patrons of Individual Souls

"See that you do not despise one of these little ones; for I tell you that in heaven their angels always behold the face of my Father who is in heaven."

— MT. 18:10

References to angels are numerous within both the Old and New Testaments of the Bible. Some of these angel verses lead us to understand that each person has his or her own private angel, a guardian angel to guide them throughout their lifetime on earth.

One verse that clearly supports this concept is Mt. 18:10, but Ps. 91:11-12 also gives us cause to believe:

For he will give his angels charge of you to guard you in all your ways. On their hands they will bear you up, lest you dash your foot against a stone.

Another verse to ponder is Heb. 1:14:

Are they not all ministering spirits sent to serve, for the sake of those who are to inherit salvation?

The word *angel* comes from the Greek word *aggelos*, which means "messenger." The primary job of all angels is to serve God, often by delivering important messages to people on earth. Guardian angels serve God by watching over their assigned individuals, often giving them subtle messages and nudges, striving to keep them safe and turned toward God throughout their lives.

The *Catechism of the Catholic Church* states: "From its beginning until death human life is surrounded by their watchful care and intercession. Beside each believer stands an angel as protector and shepherd leading him to life" (336). "The church venerates the angels who help her on her earthly pilgrimage and protect every human being" (352).

The devotion to guardian angels is an ancient one that seems to have begun in England where there is evidence of special Masses having honored these protective spirits as early as 804. Many historians consider the ancient British writer, Reginald of Canterbury, to have authored the classic prayer, *Angel of God*. It was in 1670 that Pope Clement X granted an official feast day, Oct. 2, to honor the guardian angels.

ANGEL OF GOD

Angel of God, my guardian dear,
To whom his love commits me here.
Ever this (day/night) be at my side,
To light and guard, to rule and guide.
Amen.

Ps. 91:11-12 · Mt. 18:10 · Heb. 1:14

ST. PHILIP THE DEACON

October 11
(Formerly June 6)
Patron of Apologists

Philip went down to a city of Samaria, and proclaimed to them the Christ. And the multitudes with one accord gave heed to what was said by Philip, when they heard him and saw the signs which he did.

— ACTS 8:5-6

Philip the Deacon is also known as "Philip the Evangelist" because of the amazing success he had in sharing the good news of Christ. He has been confused with Philip the Apostle at times by early Bible readers; however, a more careful analysis of Scripture reveals that they were two distinct men.

Getting a new church off the ground was an immense job for the apostles. Before long, they realized they needed help. They gathered together many believers in Jerusalem and asked them to select seven reputable men "filled with the Spirit and wisdom" to help with some of their responsibilities. Philip was one of these seven men chosen.

Shortly after this selection process, Stephen, another one of "the Seven," was stoned to death for his powerful witness to the Word. This stoning prompted many Christians to disperse, seeking safer areas, and Philip went to Samaria.

The Samaritans of the time had been greatly impressed by a magician named Simon, but Philip's powerful faith, demonstrated for all to see, quickly changed that. Astounded at the words that Philip spoke and the miracles he performed in the name of Christ, these open-hearted Samaritans dropped the magician, were baptized, and fully embraced Christianity.

Another person Philip successfully converted to Christianity was the treasurer of the Queen of Ethiopia. Philip found this Ethiopian court official reading but not understanding the writings of the propet Isaiah. Philip helped by explaining not only the words but the fulfillment of Isaiah's words as well — the life and glory of Jesus Christ. The Ethiopian was immediately won over and baptized, whereupon Philip was mystically swept away by the Spirit of the Lord.

St. Philip then traveled from town to town proclaiming Christ's news. He eventually settled in Caesarea, with his four prophetess daughters, and at one point provided lodging for Paul (and possibly Luke as well).

Acts 6:1-6 • Acts 8:4-13 • Acts 8:26-40 • Acts 21:8-9

ST. LONGINUS

October 16
(Formerly March 15)
Patron of Converts

But when they came to Jesus and saw that he was already dead,
they did not break his legs. But one of the soldiers pierced his side
with a spear, and at once there came out blood and water.

— JN. 19:33-34

Longinus is the name given to the soldier who drove a spear into the side of Jesus. The name comes from the Greek word *longche,* meaning "lance." Not a great deal of information is offered in the Bible on Longinus, but Tradition holds that he is the same person as the centurion mentioned in the other Gospels who was awestruck at the moment of Jesus's death. As the noon sunshine darkened and the earth trembled, Longinus faced Jesus and suddenly knew the truth: this gentle man nailed to the cross, now dead, was undoubtedly the innocent Son of God.

This unexpected acceptance of Jesus by the soldier and centurion Longinus is startling, at the very least. During the Crucifixion of Jesus, the Roman military in charge gave all appearances of enjoying their part in the horrendous deed. They made cruel sport of the situation, mockingly dressing Jesus in a purple robe, crafting a painful crown of thorns, and spitting on and ridiculing Him. These brutal behaviors make this spontaneous confession of faith from one of them seem miraculous.

Although many curious legends about Longinus make it difficult to verify actual truths, we can be sure of one important fact. We can celebrate with certainty that the heart of one particular soldier was transformed. Longinus openly glorified God before his demeaning comrades with a profound declaration of belief and outward conversion.

Under the beautiful dome of the Basilica of St. Peter in Rome is an enormous statue of Longinus, pensively holding his lance. It is believed that a portion of the Holy Lance — the actual lance that was imbedded within the abdomen of Christ — is securely contained within a reliquary near this inspiring image.

Jn. 19:31-37 • Mt. 27:54 • Lk. 23:47

ST. LUKE THE EVANGELIST

October 18
Patron of Artists, Doctors, Bachelors

Inasmuch as many have undertaken to compile a narrative of the things which have been accomplished among us . . . it seemed good to me also, having followed all things closely for some time past, to write an orderly account for you, most excellent Theophilus.

— LK. 1:1, 3

Luke was Gentile Greek from Syria who, although he never met Jesus personally, became a convert who made a tremendous impact on his world. Historians imply that Luke was a very talented man: a physician and a painter, fluent in at least two languages. However, his most admirable accomplishment was as a Church historian. He crafted two volumes that present the message of Christ and give a historical account of the formative years of Christianity, narratives that ultimately became the third and fifth books of the New Testament: the Gospel according to Luke, and the Acts of the Apostles.

Luke's Gospel offered an inviting and encouraging message to the Gentiles of the day, giving them reason to believe that Jesus had come for them as well as for the Jewish people. For example, it was Luke who included Holy Simeon's prophecy of Jesus being a light to the Gentiles. Also, in Chapter 17, Luke told the story of Jesus healing ten lepers, emphasizing how only the foreigner (Gentile) of the group returned to give thanks.

Luke's second volume, the Acts of the Apostles, gives a wonderful account of the efforts, struggles, and victories within the early Church after Jesus had risen from the dead. Like Luke's Gospel, the Acts of the Apostles also illustrates how Gentiles were invited to unite with Jewish believers in Christ. In addition, this book recounts much of Paul's work and travels.

Mixed in with the narratives on Paul's journeys are a few unique segments frequently called "we sections." These "we sections" have prompted many Biblical scholars to believe that Luke himself was traveling with Paul during those particular chunks of time.

We have no clear knowledge of Luke's life after his writing of these two books. Tradition states that he never married, and that he died circa A.D. 84 in Boeotia, Greece. Over time, Luke's Gospel became associated with the symbol of the ox because his Gospel starts in the Temple of Jerusalem, a place where devout Jews sometimes brought oxen as an offering to God.

Acts 1:1 • Acts 16:10-17 • Col. 4:14
2 Tim. 4:11 • Philem. 24

ST. JUDE THADDEUS

October 28
Patron of Desperate Causes, Hospitals

Judas (not Iscariot) said to him, "Lord, how is it that you will manifest yourself to us, and not to the world?" Jesus answered him, "If a man loves me, he will keep my word, and my Father will love him, and we will come to him and make our home with him."

— JN. 14:22-23

Jesus selected two apostles with the name of Judas. The English version of the name — Jude — is often used for the Judas who is also known as "Thaddeus." This Jude is not mentioned much in the Bible and has only one quote, found in Jn. 14:22. This single line was spoken during the Last Supper, a Passover meal Jesus shared with His apostles shortly before His Passion. Evidently, Jude was curious as to why Jesus would not manifest himself to the entire world. Jesus's answer seems to suggest that a life devoted to a love of truth ultimately mattered more than a revelation.

Jude Thaddeus has become a very popular saint, probably due to his patronage of hopeless cases. This patronage may stem from an experience Jude allegedly had in the city of Edessa (a city now known as Sanilurfa in modern Turkey), according to the ancient Church historian, Eusebius. Supposedly, while Jesus was still alive, Prince Agbarus of Edessa was stricken with an incurable, painful disease. The Prince heard of the miracles of Jesus and wrote Him a letter requesting a visit. Jesus responded with a promise that, in time, He would send one of His disciples. After Jesus's death and resurrection, Jude was sent to evangelize the region near Edessa and ultimately visited Agbarus. While there, Jude laid his hands upon the anguished Prince, who was instantaneously healed.

The epistle of Jude may have been written by this in-the-background apostle. This letter, written by someone named Jude, gives strong warning for believers to be cautious of false teachers.

Jude is often linked with the apostle Simon. In the lists of apostles in the New Testament, their names are listed side by side. Some legends hold that the two spent some time preaching together in Persia and that they were both martyred there, Jude by spear and Simon by saw.

Mt. 10:3 · Mk. 3:18 · Lk. 6:16
Acts 1:13 · Jn.14:15-24

ST. SIMON THE APOSTLE

October 28
Patron of Saw Workers, Tanners

And when they had entered, they went up to the upper room, where they were staying, Peter and John and James and Andrew, Philip and Thomas, Bartholomew and Matthew, James the son of Alphaeus and Simon the Zealot and Judas the son of James. All these with one accord devoted themselves to prayer.

— ACTS 1:13-14A

There are no specific stories surrounding the apostle Simon in the Bible, nor were any quotes of his recorded. He is listed merely as an apostle, although in two different ways. Matthew and Mark call him the "Cananean," while Luke identifies Simon as a "Zealot." Although the two labels sound quite different, *Cananean* is in fact derived from an Aramaic word for "zealot." Simon was probably given this title for one of two reasons: either he was full of zeal in his faith, or he belonged to a political group from the time called "Zealots."

The only information that can be gleaned from the Bible about Simon is his assumed participation in apostolic events. He was likely involved in going out to various towns to preach and heal, attending the Last Supper (but probably not the Crucifixion), seeing the risen Jesus, observing Jesus's ascension into heaven, and receiving the Holy Spirit while waiting in Jerusalem.

Beyond that, only Tradition and legend suggest any more information about Simon. It is believed that after Pentecost, he traveled extensively to spread the message of Christ. Some wrote that he preached in Syria, Egypt, Britain, Mesopotamia, and Persia — places that do indeed have evidence of early Christian influence. While in Mesopotamia, Simon reportedly met up with Jude Thaddeus. The two apostles are alleged to have traveled to Persia (Iran), and there, taught of the life of Jesus. Their words and actions were so convincing that thousands of Persians converted to Christianity. After a time, the two were martyred there: Simon was sawed into pieces, and Jude was speared to death.

Church historians record that relics of both martyred apostles were eventually brought to Rome and are now preserved in St. Peter's Basilica. This double-martyrdom story prompted Church authorities to give the two apostles a feast day to share — Oct. 28.

Mt. 10:4 • Mk. 3:18 • Lk. 6:15 • Acts 1:13

ST. APPHIA

November 22
Patroness of Altar Societies

Paul, a prisoner for Christ Jesus, and Timothy our brother, to Philemon our beloved fellow worker and Apphia our sister and Archippus our fellow soldier, and the church in your house: Grace to you and peace from God our Father and the Lord Jesus Christ.

— PHILEM. 1-3

Although this particular epistle (letter) bears the name of Philemon, it was actually addressed to three people: Philemon, Apphia, and Archippus. Apphia was likely the wife of Philemon, and many Biblical historians claim that Archippus was their son. (Paul's description of Apphia as a "sister" was meant in the sense of a sister in Christ, rather than as a blood sister.) This family lived in Colossae and was of some influence and wealth. Apphia supported the growing faith of Christianity by offering her family's home to be used as a church.

The epistle to Philemon is also known as one of Paul's four "captivity epistles," letters written while Paul was in prison. Biblical historians believe that Paul wrote to Apphia's family possibly while he was imprisoned in Rome, circa A.D. 61-63. This letter to Apphia, Philemon, and Archippus encouraged the family to forgive a runaway slave of theirs named Onesimus.

Paul (or possibly one of his brethren) also sent a letter — another captivity epistle — to all Christians of Colossae, offering sound advice and hopeful encouragement. Evidently, there were preachers in Apphia's hometown at that time who would veer off on angles, getting away from the core of Christianity — Christ. Paul gave warning in this letter against embracing these "shadow" teachings and reminded the Colossians to keep Jesus at the center of their lives. In the fourth chapter of this letter, there is a brief reference to Apphia's possible son Archippus, indicating that he was a church leader in Colossae.

It is fair to assume that Apphia read both of these epistles — Philemon and Colossians — in their entirety; they were probably also read to other new Christians in her home church. It is intriguing to consider how these letters directly influenced Apphia and her family as they continued to grow and help others grow in Christ.

Philem. 1-3 · Philem. 4-5 · Philem. 9-17
Philem. 22 · Col. 1:1-2

ST. PHILEMON

November 22
Patron of Employers

Paul, a prisoner for Christ Jesus, and Timothy our brother, to Philemon our beloved fellow worker and Apphia our sister and Archippus our fellow soldier, and the church in your house: Grace to you and peace from God our Father and the Lord Jesus Christ.

— PHILEM. 1-3

Philemon lived with two other people, Apphia and Archippus — likely, his wife and son — in Colossae (now an ancient ruin site in southwestern Turkey) during the early 60s A.D. In the New Testament epistle addressed to Philemon, Paul gives a few clues that help us understand Philemon's character.

In the greeting, Paul refers to this early Christian believer as a "beloved fellow worker." Paul also mentions Philemon's family allowing their house to be used as a church. Toward the end of the letter, Paul requests that a guest room be prepared for him at their house. These brief snippets point toward Philemon's being a faith-filled and generous man.

The crux of Paul's letter to Philemon and his family focuses on the slave, Onesimus, who fled from their home. Evidently, while on the run, Onesimus met up with Paul, who was in captivity at the time — possibly under house arrest in Rome — and who taught the runaway slave about the life and love of Jesus. After Onesimus embraced a Christian life, Paul felt it was necessary for Onesimus to return to Philemon and his family in Colossae. So he wrote his letter to Philemon, Apphia, and Archippus, encouraging them to kindly welcome and forgive their slave. Paul's words suggest that Philemon's household should not only pardon Onesimus for his action, but consider freeing him as a Christian brother. It is not recorded in the Bible how Onesimus's return was actually handled. However, it has been written that an increased Christian spirit settled in, which prompted Philemon to forgive and free the slave.

Tradition relates that Philemon and Apphia were martyred at their home in Colossae. They share Nov. 22 as a feast day.

Philem. 1-5 • Philem. 7-17 • Col. 1:1-2
Col. 4:1 • Col. 4:9

ST. ANDREW THE APOSTLE

November 30
Patron of Fishermen, Amalfi (Italy),
Unmarried Women

One of the two who heard John speak, and followed him, was Andrew, Simon Peter's brother. He first found his brother Simon, and said to him, "We have found the Messiah" (which means Christ).

— JN. 1:40-41

Andrew was a fisherman and a disciple of John the Baptist before becoming an apostle of Jesus. According to John's Gospel, Andrew was one of the first to understand that Jesus was the Messiah and eagerly ran to share the wonderful news with his brother, Simon Peter.

Andrew's name is specifically mentioned in a handful of Gospel stories. Jesus performed one of his earlier miracles in Andrew's presence: when Peter's mother-in-law was very sick. Andrew, along with his brother Peter and fellow apostles James and John, told Jesus about it. Jesus went to her, grasped her hand, and healed her illness — so completely that she got up to serve them!

The well-known story of the multiplication of the loaves and fish is found in all four gospels; however, it is John's Gospel that sheds some light onto Andrew's presence at this miraculous event. A large crowd of people — five thousand, according to John — followed Jesus to a mountain near the

Sea of Galilee. As it became obvious that there might be a problem feeding the thousands of followers, it was Andrew who let Jesus know that there was a boy with five barley loaves and two fish. Jesus collected the bread and fish and began passing out portions of the food . . . and all had enough.

John also recorded a brief encounter Andrew had with some Greeks who were very curious about Jesus. They asked Philip about the possibilities of meeting Jesus, who in turn asked Andrew, who went directly to Jesus with the request. Jesus's reply seems to have indicated the eventual inclusion of Gentiles among his followers.

What Andrew did after receiving the Holy Spirit at Pentecost is not certain, but legends hold that he preached in Asia Minor and Greece. Tradition tells us that Andrew was martyred in Patras, Greece, on an X-shaped cross. In the 1200s, the Crusaders took his remains from Constantinople to Amalfi, Italy. Many claim that his arm bones are venerated in Scotland.

Mt. 4:18-20 • Jn. 1:35-44 • Mk. 1:29-31
Jn. 6:8-9 • Jn. 12:20-22

ST. STEPHEN

December 26
Patron of Deacons, Masons,
Headache Sufferers

*And as they were stoning Stephen, he prayed, "Lord Jesus, receive
my spirit." And he knelt down and cried with a loud voice,
"Lord, do not hold this sin against them." And when he had said
this, he fell asleep.*

— ACTS 7:59-60

In the early days of the Church, after Jesus sent the Holy
Spirit upon His disciples, the apostles went about Jerusalem preaching and performing many miracles and signs of
wonder. New believers were joining the way of Jesus in great
numbers. Before long, the apostles realized that they needed
help in taking care of such a rapidly growing community.
They searched out seven men known to be wise and devout
to assist with certain duties, freeing the apostles up for prayer
and ministry. Stephen was one of the seven chosen.

It soon became evident that Stephen was an extraordinary preacher and could work great marvels, bringing even
more people to the new way of faith. Unfortunately, Stephen's
holy persuasiveness seriously irritated some religious zealots.
They spread lies about him, gathered together some false wit-
nesses, and brought him before the Sanhedrin.

When Stephen was asked to speak by the council, he
reminded the synagogue authorities of the countless persecu-

tions of holy prophets throughout Israelite history. Bravely comparing those persecutions to the behavior of the Sanhedrin, he accused them of denying words of truth. The council members were livid over Stephen's speech. Stephen then gazed upward and described a vision of heaven with Jesus at the right hand of God — an action that sent his audience over the edge; they brought him out of the city and began to stone him. As the stones were hurled at him, causing an excruciating death, Stephen spoke gentle words of prayer and forgiveness.

Stephen's death created an unexpected boost to the mission of Christ. All Christians in Jerusalem were then so heavily persecuted by Jewish leaders that many fled to other cities, towns, and countries. These scattered disciples taught people in their new places about the message and life of Jesus, and multitudes were converted. So, this dispersion of believers brought about by the martyrdom of Stephen was actually an early step in making Christianity a universal faith.

Acts 6:1-6 • Acts 6:8-15 • Acts 7:1-50
Acts 7:51-60 • Acts 8:1-2

ST. JOHN THE EVANGELIST

December 27
Patron of Writers, Booksellers, Friendships

When Jesus saw his mother, and the disciple whom he loved standing near, he said to his mother, "Woman, behold, your son!" Then he said to the disciple, "Behold, your mother!" And from that hour the disciple took her to his own home.

— JN. 19:26-27

John, both an apostle and an Evangelist, played a very prominent role in many New Testament narratives. John was part of an inner-circle trio with his brother James (the Greater) and Peter, partaking in privileged incidents with Jesus — the raising of Jairus's daughter, the Transfiguration, and the agony at Gethsemane — while the other nine were elsewhere.

John and his brother James were nicknamed "Sons of Thunder" by Jesus. Exactly why they were given this title is not explained. However, the two brothers did exhibit at least two instances of audacious behavior: wanting to bring fire from heaven down upon the Samaritans who refused to listen to the message of Christ, and asking Jesus for great places of honor in heaven.

Within the Gospel of John, there are five different references to "the disciple whom Jesus loved" (13:23, 19:26, 20:2, 21:7, 21:20). Over the centuries, the vast majority of Biblical scholars have deemed this beloved disciple to be John himself.

These mysterious references actually point to a less-thunderous personality; for example, the beloved disciple resting his head on Jesus's chest at the Last Supper, and Jesus requesting that the beloved disciple take care of his mother, Mary.

Tradition places John in Ephesus (in modern Turkey) after Pentecost, where he cared for Mary and probably wrote the fourth Gospel. John's Gospel stands out from the other three, offering a uniquely embellished portrayal of Christ. This Gospel is symbolized with an eagle due to its "soaring" theological style.

It is probable that either John himself or a disciple of his wrote the three epistles of John. Many claim that he also wrote the book of Revelation, a work chock-full of mystical imagery, during an exile on the island of Patmos.

John is believed to have lived to an old age and died of natural causes. A basilica in Ephesus at one time reportedly held his remains, but that church is now in ruins.

Mt. 4:21-22 · Mk. 5:37 · Lk. 9:28-29 · Mk. 14:32-34
Lk. 9:54-55 · Mk. 10:35-41

THE HOLY INNOCENTS

December 28
Patrons of Babies, Children's Choirs

Then Herod, when he saw that he had been tricked by the wise men, was in a furious rage, and he sent and killed all the male children in Bethlehem and in all that region who were two years old or under, according to the time which he had ascertained from the wise men.

— Mt. 2:16

The three wise men (or Magi) who traveled from points east, searching out a newborn king, elicited a feverish scare in King Herod the Great. This irascible ruler of Judea was very easily threatened; he'd had some of his own sons, a wife, mother-in-law, an uncle, and other relatives killed out of fury and suspicion.

King Herod the Great tried to trick the Magi by falsely expressing an interest in the new king and indicating that he would like to pay homage as well. He requested that the three men return to Jerusalem after they had found the child to let him know of the babe's specific whereabouts within Bethlehem. Meanwhile, he was already forming a plan to eliminate this new threat.

When he realized that the Magi were not going to return with this information, he made a drastic decision: to have all baby boys aged two and younger in Bethlehem and the surrounding areas killed. By this, he erroneously supposed (for

Joseph had already taken Mary and Jesus away from Bethlehem), he would be certain to kill the one destined to become king. This cruel action, and the anguish it caused, had been foreshadowed by the prophet Jeremiah's words about Jacob's wife, Rachel . . . weeping inconsolably for her children, who were no more.

These baby boys are considered by many to be the first martyrs of the Christian faith, the first to die for — and this time exclusively, *instead of* — Christ. Many have called these little fellows "flowers of the martyrs" because of their special place in Christian martyrdom. In the early fifth century, a man named Aurelius Prudentius wrote a hymn in honor of these babies called *Salvete, Flores Martyrum* ("Hail, Flowers of the Martyrs"):

Hail, tender wreath of flowers, whose day
of beauty, crossed by tyrant spite,
Was offered, as a budding spray
of roses to the Lord of light.

Yours was the foremost glory given
To martyrdom, O shining throng,
Ye play amid the halls of Heaven
With palm and crown in holy song.

Mt. 2:13 · Mt. 2:16-18 · Jer. 31:15

SAINTS IN THE BIBLE

SAINT	MEANING OF NAME	FEAST DAY	PATRONAGE	BIBLICAL REFERENCE
Mary, the Blessed Mother	Beloved	Jan. 1	Motherhood, Nuns, Aviators; Protection During Storms	Lk.1:30-31
Timothy	Honoring God	Jan. 26	Stomach Disorder Sufferers	Acts 16:1-3
Titus	Safe	Jan. 26	Crete	2 Cor. 7:5-6
Holy Simeon	Listening	Feb. 3 (10/8)	Elderly	Lk. 2:25
Onesimus the Slave	Useful	Feb. 15 (2/16)	Discouraged Employees	Philem.10-12
Joseph	He Will Add	Mar. 19	Fathers, Workers, A Peaceful Death	Mt. 1:20-21
Dismas the Good Thief	Dying	Mar. 25	Prisoners, Repentant Thieves, Penitent Criminals	Lk. 23:41-42
Mary of Clopas	Beloved	Apr. 24 (4/9)	Caretakers	Jn. 19:25
Mark the Evangelist	Large Hammer	Apr. 25	Lawyers, Venice, Stained Glass Workers	2 Tim. 4:11b
Simon of Jerusalem	Listening	Apr. 27 (2/18)	Bishops	Mt. 13:55
James the Less	Supplanter	May 3	Pharmacists, Unnoticed People	Acts 1:13-14a
Philip the Apostle	Friend of Horses	May 3	Hatmakers, Pastry Chefs	Jn.1:43

SAINT	MEANING OF NAME	FEAST DAY	PATRONAGE	BIBLICAL REFERENCE
Matthias the Apostle	Gift of God	May 14	Alcoholism Sufferers, Tailors, Carpenters	Acts 1:26
Barnabas	Son of Encouragement	June 11	Peacemaking; Protection from Hailstorms	Acts 4:36-37
John the Baptist	Yahweh Is Gracious	June 24	Baptism, Converts, Convulsion Sufferers	Lk.1:43-44
Paul	Humble	June 29	Writers, Musicians, Lay People	Acts 22:7-8
Peter the Apostle	Rock	June 29	Fishermen, Calmness, Clockmakers	Mt. 16:18-19
Thomas the Apostle	Twin	July 3	Architects	Jn. 20:28
Aquila and Priscilla	Eagle & Ancient	July 8	Married Couples	Acts 18:1-2a
Jason	To Heal	July 12	Guest Keepers	Acts 17:6
Silas	Forest	July 13	Assistants	Acts 16:25-26
Joseph Barsabbas	He Will Add	July 20	Quiet Holiness	Acts 1:21, 22b-23
Mary Magdalene	Beloved	July 22	Penitent Sinners, Contemplative Life	Jn. 20:15-16
The Three Wise Men		July 24 (7/23)	Traveling, Fever Sufferers; Against Sudden Death	Mt. 2:10-11

SAINT	MEANING OF NAME	FEAST DAY	PATRONAGE	BIBLICAL REFERENCE
James the Greater	Supplanter	July 25	Spain, Arthritics, Soldiers, Pharmacists	Mt. 4:21-22
Lazarus	God Is My Helper	July 29 (12/17)	Emergency Medical Technicians	Jn. 11:43-44
Martha	Lady of the House	July 29	Homemakers, Servants, Unmarried Women	Jn.11:27
Bartholomew (Nathanael) the Apostle	God Has Given	Aug. 24	Butchers, Calmness, Leatherworkers	Jn.1:48-49
Joseph of Arimathea	He Will Add	Aug. 31 (3/17)	Undertakers, Pallbearers	Mk.15:42-43
Phoebe	Pure, Bright	Sept. 3	Women's Ministries	Rom. 16:1-2
Matthew the Apostle	Gift of God	Sept. 21	Bankers, Accountants	Mt. 9:9
Elizabeth	God Is My Oath	Sept. 23 (11/5)	Expectant Mothers	Lk. 1:41-42
Zechariah	Yahweh Remembers	Sept. 23 (11/5)	Fathers-to-Be	Lk.1:13, 14
Gabriel the Archangel	God Is Strong	Sept. 29	Communication Arts	Lk. 1:26-28
Michael the Archangel	Who Is Like God?	Sept. 29	Paratroopers, Artists, A Holy Death	Dan. 12:1

SAINT	MEANING OF NAME	FEAST DAY	PATRONAGE	BIBLICAL REFERENCE
Raphael the Archangel	God Heals	Sept. 29	Young People, Peacefulness, Healing	Tob. 5:10
Guardian Angels		Oct. 2	Individual Souls	Mt. 18:10
Philip the Deacon	Friend of Horses	Oct. 11 (6/6)	Apologists	Acts 8:5-6
Longinus	Lance	Oct. 16 (3/15)	Converts	Jn. 19:33-34
Luke the Evangelist	Light	Oct. 18	Artists, Doctors, Bachelors	Lk.1:1, 3
Jude Thaddeus	Praised	Oct. 28	Desperate Causes, Hospitals	Jn. 14:22-23
Simon the Apostle	Listening	Oct. 28	Saw Workers, Tanners	Acts 1:13-14a
Apphia	Increasing	Nov. 22	Altar Societies	Philem. 1-3
Philemon	Affectionate	Nov. 22	Employers	Philem. 1-3
Andrew the Apostle	Manly	Nov. 30	Fishermen, Amalfi (Italy), Unmarried Women	Jn. 1:40-41
Stephen	Crown	Dec. 26	Deacons, Masons, Headache Sufferers	Acts 7:59-60
John the Evangelist	Yahweh Is Gracious	Dec. 27	Writers, Booksellers, Friendships	Jn. 19:26-27
The Holy Innocents		Dec. 28	Babies, Children's Choirs	Mt. 2:16

BIBLIOGRAPHY

Achtemeier, Paul, Ed. *Harper's Bible Dictionary*. New York: HarperCollins, 1985.

Attwater, Donald, and John Cumming. *A New Dictionary of Saints*. Collegeville, MN: The Liturgical Press, 1993.

Baybrooke, Marcus, and James Harpus. *The Collegeville Atlas of the Bible*. Collegeville, MN: The Liturgical Press, 1999.

Benedict XVI, Pope, Ed. (James Cardinal Gibbons, Imprimatur). *The Roman Martyrology Published by Order of Gregory XIII*. Baltimore, MD: John Murphy and Co. Publishers, 1897.

Brown, Raymond Edward, Joseph A. Fitzmyer, and Ronald E. Murphy, Eds. *The New Jerome Biblical Commentary*. Englewood Cliffs, NJ: Prentice Hall, 1990.

Calamari, Barbara, and Sandra DiPasqua. *Holy Cards*. New York: Harry N. Abrams, Inc., 2004.

———. *Visions of Mary*. New York: Harry N. Abrams, Inc., 2004.

Cowan, Tom. *The Way of the Saints*. New York: G.P. Putnam's Sons, 1998.

Cruz, Joan Carroll. *Relics*. Huntington, IN: Our Sunday Visitor, Inc., 1983.

Cunial, Hector (Imprimatur). *The New World Dictionary Concordance to the New American Bible*. Charlotte, NC: C. D. Stampley Enterprises, Inc., 1970.

Dwyer, John C. *Church History: Twenty Centuries of Catholic Christianity*. Mahwah, NJ: Paulist Press, 1985.

Eusebius, translated by C.F. Cruse. *Eusebius's Ecclesiastical History*. Peabody, MA: Hendrickson Publishers, 2004.

Gardner, Joseph L., Ed. *Who's Who in the Bible*. Pleasantville, NY: The Reader's Digest Association, 1994.

Gitlitz, David, and Linda Davidson. *The Pilgrimage Road to Santiago*. New York: St. Martin's Press, 2000.

Harrington, Rt. Rev. Msgr. John H., Ed. *The Catholic Encyclopedia for School and Home*. Yonkers, NY: St. Joseph's Seminary and College, 1965.

Hoever, Rev. Hugo, Ed. *Lives of the Saints*. New York: Catholic Book Publishing Co., 1989.

Kleinz, Msgr. John. *The Who's Who of Heaven: Saints for All Seasons*. Westmeinster, MD: Christian Classics, 1989.

Lord, Bob and Penny. *Heavenly Army of Angels*. Slidell, LA: Journeys of Faith, 1991.

————. *Saint Paul* (VHS). Slidell, LA: Journeys of Faith, 1990.

Luce, Clare Boothe, Ed. *Saints for Now*. San Francisco: Ignatius Press, 1993.

Lukefahr, Oscar, C.M. *A Catholic Guide to the Bible*. Liguori, MO: Liguori Publications, 1998.

Lunghi, Cherie (narrator). *Mystery of the Three Kings*. London: Atlantic Productions, 2002.

Martyrologium Romanum. Editio Altera, Civitate Vaticana, 2004.

Parente, Fr. Alessio, O.F.M. Cap. *"Send Me Your Guardian Angel" Padre Pio*. Barto, PA: National Centre For Padre Pio, Inc., 1983.

Ratzinger, Joseph Cardinal (Imprimi Potest). *Catechism of the Catholic Church*. New York: Doubleday, 1995.

Ruffin, Bernard. *The Twelve: The Lives of the Apostles After Calvary*. Huntington, IN: Our Sunday Visitor, Inc., 1997.

Senior, Donald, Ed. *The Catholic Study Bible*. New York: Oxford University Press, 1990.

Stevens, Rev. Clifford. *The One Year Book of Saints*. Huntington, IN: Our Sunday Visitor, Inc., 1989.

Stravinskas, Peter, M.J., Ed. *Catholic Encyclopedia*. Huntington, IN: Our Sunday Visitor Publishing Division, 1991.

Then and Now Bible Map Book. Necedah, WI: Ascension Press of Rose Publishing, Inc., 2003.

Walsh, Michael. *Book of Saints*. Mystic, CT: Twenty-Third Publications, 1995.

————, Ed. *Butler's Lives of the Saints*. San Francisco: HarperCollins Publishers, 1991.

INTERNET

http://198.62.75.1/www1/ofm/sites/TScpsyEN.html
http://saints.sqpn.com
www.americancatholic.org
www.answers.com
www.behindthename.com
www.biblehistory.net
www.bibleplaces.com
www.catholic-forum.com
www.catholic.org
www.catholicfirst.com
www.christusrex.org
www.enjoyturkey.com
www.gargano.it
www.gospelcom.net
www.holylandphotos.org
www.hymnsandcarolsofchristmas.com
www.ichrusa.com/saintsalive/euro.htm
www.monum.fr
www.magnificat.ca
www.newadvent.org
www.sacred-destinations.com

Our Sunday Visitor ...
Your Source for Discovering the Riches of the Catholic Faith

Our Sunday Visitor has an extensive line of materials for young children, teens, and adults. Our books, Bibles, pamphlets, CD-ROMs, audios, and videos are available in bookstores worldwide.

To receive a FREE full-line catalog or for more information, call **Our Sunday Visitor** at **1-800-348-2440, ext. 3**. Or write **Our Sunday Visitor** / 200 Noll Plaza / Huntington, IN 46750.

Please send me ____ A catalog
Please send me materials on:
____ Apologetics and catechetics
____ Prayer books
____ The family
____ Reference works
____ Heritage and the saints
____ The parish

Name _____
Address _____ Apt._____
City _____ State _____ Zip_____
Telephone ( ) _____

A91BBBBF

Please send a friend ____ A catalog
Please send a friend materials on:
____ Apologetics and catechetics
____ Prayer books
____ The family
____ Reference works
____ Heritage and the saints
____ The parish

Name _____
Address _____ Apt._____
City _____ State _____ Zip_____
Telephone ( ) _____

A91BBBBP

OurSundayVisitor
200 Noll Plaza, Huntington, IN 46750
Toll free: **1-800-348-2440**
Website: www.osv.com